Ecocriticism
Vital Concerns of Ecology in Critical Theory

Govind Digambar Kokane

ATLANTIC
PUBLISHERS & DISTRIBUTORS (P) LTD

ATLANTIC
PUBLISHERS & DISTRIBUTORS (P) LTD
7/22, Ansari Road, Darya Ganj, New Delhi
Tel.: +91-11-4077 5252, 2327 3880
E-mail: orders@atlanticbooks.com
Web: www.atlanticbooks.com

This edition published in 2022 by Atlantic Publishers & Distributors (P) Ltd.

Reprint 2025

Printed & bound in India by Atlantic Print Services

Dedication

The book has been dedicated to
My Philosophical Mother
Sharda Digambar Kokane
and
Social Activist Father
Digambar Lakshman Kokane

Acknowledgements

I express profound gratitude to my research guide, Dr. Mabel Fernandes, Professor, Department of English, Dr. Babasaheb Ambedkar Marathwada University, Aurangabad, Maharashtra, for her splendid supervision and guidance. I express deep gratitude to Professor Pramod Yeole (Vice Chancellor), Prof. Shyam Shirsath (Pro Vice Chancellor), and Prof. Jaishree Suryawanshi (Registrar) of Dr. Babasaheb Ambedkar Marathwada University, Aurangabad, for their motivation and encouragement for research. I am thankful to Dr. Dhanraj Mane, Director, Higher Education, Maharashtra, for providing cooperation and inspiration. The teachers have been an inspiration to me; especially I want to thank Dr. R.M. Sangewar for providing inspiration and direction. I want to express my insightful sense of gratitude to Prof. Dattatraya Gaikwad (Director, Dr. B.A.M.U., Sub-campus, Osmanabad) for his cooperation and encouragement. I am deeply thankful to former Directors of Sub-campus, Dr. Ramesh Dapke, Dr. Ashok Mohekar, Dr. Jaisingrao Deshmukh, Dr. Anar Salunke, Dr. Prashant Dixit; and former Academic Director of Sub-campus, Dr. Arun Kharat for providing constant motivation and necessary infrastructure for my research. I express philosophical gratitude to Prof. Ramesh Chougule, Head, Department of English, Dr. Babasaheb Ambedkar Marathwada University Sub-campus, Osmanabad, who has provided me valuable suggestions, cooperation, and encouragement. I am thankful to Prof. Uttam Ambhore, Head, Department of English, Dr. B.A.M.U., Aurangabad, for his guidance and cooperation. I also thank all faculty members of the Department of English for their timely help and inspiration. I express gratitude to Deputy Registrar at Sub-campus, Dr. Vishnu Karale for his valuable suggestions.

For thoughtful and much appreciated advice, I am grateful to Prof. A.B. Indalkar, Dr. S.D. Pawar, Dr. A.B. Kadam, Dr. Umesh Kamble, and Prof. Ashwin Munde. The Department of English,

Dr. Babasaheb Ambedkar Marathwada University, Aurangabad and Department of English at Sub-campus, Osmanabad have always provided me marvellous research support and an equally marvellous critical audience of colleagues and post-graduate students. I thank all of them for their valuable feedbacks. I take this opportunity to thank my colleagues, Mr. S.S. Salunke, Mr. H.P. Garad, Mr. V.G. Bhoval, Mr. Chavan Kamlakar, Mr. R.R. Pawar, Mr. V.P. Agale, and administrative assistant Mr. R.S. Mahajan for their kind assistance. I am thankful to my brother-in law Mr. Shankar Konapure for providing motivation and inspiration.

I am grateful to the Central Library, Jawaharlal Nehru University, New Delhi; Indira Gandhi Memorial Library, University of Hyderabad, Hyderabad; Osmania University, Hyderabad; Central University of English and Foreign Languages, Hyderabad; and Central Library, Dr. Babasaheb Ambedkar Marathwada University, Aurangabad, and Sub-campus Osmanabad for providing opportunity to use their print and e-resources for my research.

I am greatly indebted to my family for their support and encouragement. I deeply thank my parents for their encouragement and motivation. I am blessed with brilliant brothers, Nagnath Digambar Kokane, teacher at Zilla Parishad School, Narsi Tanda, Tq. Naigaon, Dist. Nanded, Balaji Digambar Koakne, Assistant Professor at Department of Chemistry, Kumarswami Mahavidyalaya, Ausa, Dist. Latur, and Aakash Digamabar Koakne, Sarpanch, Chitmogra Gram Panchayat, Tq. Biloli, Dist. Nanded; and sisters, Chitra Digambar Kokane and Hema Digambar Kokane. I thank them for their inspiration and encouragement. Closest to home as always my foremost debt is to my wife Ira, whose confidence and encouragement, motivation, and determination have inspired me. I thank my children Anushka and Omkar for their endurance, happiness, resilience, and cooperation.

I am thankful to Atlantic Publishers and Distributors Pvt. Ltd., New Delhi, for insightful and detailed reviews. I appreciate their efforts and cooperation.

Govind Digambar Kokane

Preface

Ecocriticism is the most relevant field of literary and cultural study in the twenty first century. The present book aims at a detailed study of it. It organizes its material in terms of introduction, Cheryll Glotfelty, Harold Fromm, and Lawrence Buell. The last chapter concludes the study of the theory and practice of ecocriticism, and recommends further reading.

Ecocriticism started developing in the 1990s. Cheryll Glotfelty is the founder of Ecocriticism. William Rueckert coined the term Ecocriticism in 1978. It is the study of the literature and the environment. It is the theory committed to effect change in the world by analyzing the cultural, social, artistic, economic, political, and ideological functions of the nature which contribute to development of the world. Ecocriticism has expressed concern to examine ourselves and the world around us. It analyses the way we represent, interact with, and construct the environment. It is unique in its analysis of the interaction between nature and human nature. It is the literary response to the most pressing contemporary issue of all, the global environmental crisis. It redefines our relationship with the nature and environment.

Human culture is intimately connected with the physical environment. Ecocriticism explores the roots of the problem of ecological crisis in the relationship of society with the nature and the structure of the society within. It also explores the need of the economic and social justice for the formation of a cohesive society. It is a well acknowledged truth that quality of natural environment determines the quality of human life. We can overcome the global environmental crisis, with the right understanding and observation of our ethical system. Ecocritics analyse texts that illustrate environmental concerns.

Ecocriticism analyses the interdependence of human life and non-human life. It analyses the close relationship between nature and culture. It analyses the representation of human life and nature in literary texts. It examines the role of physical setting in the plot of the novel, drama, and short story. Characters are ecologically situated. Our cultural, academic, economic, and political development is basically connected with the biodiversity and nature. Self realization involves the transformation not only from ego to social self but also from social self to ecological self. Nature plays a vital role in shaping human attitudes and behaviours.

Ecocriticism is committed to bring economic, social, political, and cultural justice all over the world. The world needs an alternative approach of development that is sustainable development. The development pattern should create social cohesion rather than social inequality. Equality and inclusiveness strengthen the community. It increases the bond between the individual and the society. Free market mechanisms are responsible for breaking down of the traditional cultural values. The sustainable development is the best model of development which improves the standard of life for all.

Cheryll Glotfelty, Harold Fromm, and Lawrence Buell are well known critics in the field of ecocriticism. The book provides a detailed analysis of their immense and valuable contribution to the theory and practice of ecocriticism. It analyses the critical works of three leading writers and thinkers in the field of ecocriticism. It offers a comprehensive array of perspectives on the new approach of ecological criticism. It explores the organic interrelationship between human life and nature. It investigates ecological values in literary works. Healthy environment is necessary for a strong society. Human culture and civilization develop on the strong foundation of nature. Ecocriticism envisions an ecologically sustainable human society. It analyses how literature has affected human and non-human relationships. It analyses literature from the environmental perspectives. It provides the valuable and profound insights for the sustainable development, organic society, and the world based on the ethical values of liberty, equality, and fraternity.

It is the standard theory, relevant in the contemporary times and, also, important in all times. The quality of natural environment determines the quality of human life. Imagination and creativity are powerful forces which establish understanding with nature. Respect is cognitive as well as moral virtue. To treat something with respect involves knowledge. Spirituality and ethics determine our attitude towards nature. Nature sustains the human life. Ecocriticism expresses a deep concern for the harmonious relationship between human life and nature. All works, real or fictional, take place in an environment that is setting. Environment impacts characters and actions of the present and successive generations. Ecocriticism opposes all kinds of injustices and exploitation. It focuses on the qualities of human life and the environment. It links concerns of social justice to concerns of environmental quality. Environmental problems are inseparable from other political, social, economic, and cultural problems. Environment affects every aspect of human life. Ecocriticism provides the valuable insights to establish and maintain the social and the environmental justice. It has strengthened the close association of human life and nature. The organic social culture is always sensitive to the natural world. It investigates ecological values. It examines the concept of nature. It evaluates human perception of wilderness. It describes environmental issues in popular culture and modern literature. The relationship between nature and human life is organic. Human culture and civilization develop on the strong foundation of nature. Ecocriticism is a distinct critical school or movement. It is a revolutionary theory of literature. It has strong ethical aspects. It relates literature to the natural environment. Study of literature ideally inspires political activism. Ecocriticism provides the theory for environmental, economic, social, political, and cultural justice. It presents the important relationship between nature and culture.

Govind Digambar Kokane

Contents

1
Introduction

The field of literary criticism and theory is dynamic and heterogeneous. Ecocriticism is unique amongst contemporary literary and cultural theories. It is a new critical discipline. It is a celebratory discourse. It emerged as a literary theory. It is the study of the relationship between nature and human nature. It explores the relationships between literature and the environment. Man is part of the Nature. Literature and art influence human life. Human life too influences the art and literature. Ecocriticism redefines our relationship with the environment and Nature. It identifies roots of the problem of ecological crisis in relationship of the society with nature and the structure of the society within. It is also related with social and economic justice. The loss of ecology has irreversible, inter-generational consequences. The protection of air, water, soil health, and biodiversity should be primary environmental imperatives.

Environment impacts people's day today lives. Quality of natural environment determines the quality of human life. Cultural survival of people depends upon integrated environmental practices. Imagination and creativity are powerful forces which establish understanding with nature. There is the need to increase the environmental awareness among the people of all countries.

The arrival of ecocriticism is as timely as it is necessary. The environmental historian Donald Worster suggests:

> We are facing a global crisis today, not because of how ecosystems function, but rather because of how our ethical

> systems function. To overcome that crisis, we need to understand those ethical systems and use that understanding to reform them. (Donald, Worster, *Wealth of Nature: Environmental History and the Ecological Imagination*, p. 27)[1]

The study of literature and the environment has been around in one form or other since the beginning of literary studies. The field of ecocriticism has taken complete shape recently. Several pioneering studies in the 1950s and 1960s established a foundation for the field. Ecocriticism has become a coherent and organized discipline within literary studies in the last decade of twentieth century. The publication of two landmark books in 1996, *The Ecocriticism Reader,* edited by Cheryll Glotfelty and Harold Fromm and Lawrence Buell's *The Environmental Imagination* are breakthroughs in the field of ecological criticism. Ecocriticism, a critical approach began in the USA in the late 1980s and in the UK in the early 1990s. The transcendentalists, Ralph Waldo Emerson (1803-82), Margaret Fuller (1810-50), and Henry David Thoreau (1817-62) have exerted great influence on eco centred writing in America. They launched the first major literary movement in America Transcendentalism to achieve cultural independence from European models. Thoreau's *Walden* is the classic account of the coming out of modern life to renew the self by establishing close kinship between nature and self. Emerson's first short book, *Nature* is a collection of reflective essays on the impact upon him of the natural world.

United Kingdom version of ecocriticism is known as Green Studies. The Green Studies takes its bearings from the Romanticism of the 1790s. Jonathan Bate, the critic, is the founding figure of Green Studies. He is the author of *Romantic Ecology: Wordsworth and the Environmental Tradition.* He has also written *The Song of the Earth*. Soper Kate's *What is Nature? Culture, Politics, and the Non-Human* is a fundamental text which laid the foundations of contemporary ecocriticism. Many of the concerns of the ecocriticism are evident in Raymond William's book, *The Country and the City*. Lawrence Coupe edited *The Green Studies Reader: From Romanticism to Ecocriticism.*

The Green Studies and Ecocriticism both are linked in their approaches and aims. But they differ in origin and prominence. Generally, ecocriticism is a preferred term in America whereas green study is frequently used in the United Kingdom. British critics warn us of environmental threats come from governmental, industrial, commercial, and neo-colonial forces. Bate argues in *The Song of the Earth* that colonialism and deforestation have regularly gone together.

Ecocriticism is concerned with the decisive matter of the relationship between culture and nature. Eco critics reject the notion that everything is socially and/or linguistically constructed. Eco critics firmly believe that Nature affects human life. Sri Aurobindo believed:

> For all problems of existence are essentially problems of harmony. They arise from the perception of an unsolved discord and the instinct of an undiscovered agreement or unity. (*The Future Evolution of Man,* p. 1)[2]

Ecocriticism is concerned with the environmental implications of literary texts. Any literary work can be analysed from the ecological perspective. Analytical frameworks developed in other disciplines can be incorporated into an ecocritical reading. Human and non-human life is interdependent. Ecocriticism analyses the representation of humans and their environment in eco drama. Traditionally human centered perspective dominated drama scholarship and performance. Humans live in a mutually reliant system. Human and land, animals, plants, trees influence one another. Ecocriticism posits a radical rethinking about the representation of humans and their environment. It offers fresh insights into cultural and political ideologies which are the foundation of some of the pressing social and environmental issues of the past and the present. It challenges the ideological structures that create and perpetuate social and environmental injustices. It supports organic farming. It favours sustainable development. It exposes dominant ideologies which are responsible for ecological crisis. Characters are ecologically situated whether it is play or a novel. Downing Cless's article, "Ecologically Conjuring

Doctor Faustus" presents an eco-critical reading of Christopher Marlowe's *Doctor Faustus*. Cless analysed the play from the perspective of natural philosophy. Cless argues that the play is more than a morality tale; it is not just about hunger for power. The play is Marlowe's commentary on "over-extending, over-consuming, and over-reaching" (Cless, *Journal of Dramatic Theory and Criticism*, Spring 2006).[3] Doctor Faustus is an explicitly independent character, who is selfish. Therefore, he lacks communion with nature. The self-centeredness has made him tragic-anti-hero. Generally, he is assumed to be a tragic hero but he does not rise to be a tragic hero because of his utter selfishness. In this regard Des Jardins says:

> The flourishing of human life and culture depends on the protection of the natural environment. Nature has its own intrinsic value, dignity, and beauty. Pollution, loss of natural resources and reduction of biological diversity have dire consequences for human and non-human life.
>
> Green political thinkers criticize the indiscriminate economic growth. They are committed for qualitative or ecologically sustainable growth. Economic policy should raise meaningful quality of life for the people. Green politics addresses the issue of growing gap between rich and poor, the undermining of life support services and a diminishment in the overall quality of life for everyone. It holds the political goal of achieving greater social and environmental equity, greater democratic control of social and economic life. It supports greater decentralization of political power. It expresses strong concerns for political and environmental justice. The nature of representation is one of the important concerns of literary theory. The study of literature has always been conducted in a spirit of advocacy of natural and democratic values. It is against hierarchical and artificial values. American writers in the Renaissance cared the natural and democratic values the most. The anthropocentric view of the world has many implications for the environment. How does human view the nature determines their relationship to nature. Human activities are responsible for degradation of rivers. Deep Ecology views anthropocentrism as the main cause of the

> environmental crisis. Social ecology views "specific human institutions and practices—*unjust* institutions and practices" are the main causes of the crisis. (Des Jardins, 235)[4]

Naess is the father of deep ecology. He presented an ecological world view. The notion of selfhood is based on active identification with wider and wider circles of being. The self is not a fixed entity, but a cultivated one. Our economic, social and cultural development is basically connected with the biodiversity and Nature. He says, "That is we identify not merely with our family, our community, our culture, or with humanity as a whole, but also with our immediate environment, the place where we are born or to which we belong, our land, our earth" (Naess). In this way Naess envisages self-realisation as involving the transition not only from ego to social self, but from social self to ecological self.

Nature writing has emerged as a powerful force in contemporary literature. David W. Orr argues in *Ecological Literacy: Education and the Transition to a Postmodern World* (1992) that liberal arts play a crucial role in helping humanity to respond to the crisis of sustainability. Literary artists have been exploring the relationship between human culture and the natural world. Harold Fromm argues that ecocriticism is rooted in the past:

> Like Moliere's M. Jourdain speaking prose without knowing it, classic writers were unwittingly doing ecocriticism for centuries before the genre burst forth onto the academic scene in the early 1990s. From Virgil's *Georgics* to John Clare to Thoreau to Rachel Carson, sensitive people had actually noticed that they were living on and from the primal mud of Earth. (Harold Fromm, Review Essay)[5]

Twenty-first century is often called as the century of the environment. Ecocriticism is a coherent and broadly based movement. Without biosphere and planetary conditions human life could not exist. Ecocriticism challenges too much postmodern critical discourses as well as to the critical systems of the past. Our perceptions of nature are necessarily human constructed. Nature plays a vital role in shaping human attitudes and behaviour. Literary work has the environmental context. Charles Darwin asserted in *The Descent of Man* and *Selection in Relation to Sex* that humans are descended from earlier forms of life. Human differ in degree only from other animals. Literature is related to nature and human life. Humans have to take prompt and vigorous actions to check the pollution and spoliation affecting the planet earth. Our efforts should be strong to protect the Earth's ecosystems to safeguard our future on the planet. Political leaders should understand the depth of the environmental concerns for the sustainable development of the country. We should not assess our wellbeing just in economic terms. We should assess progress not just in terms of fiscal loss and gain but in terms of earth's biological and cultural loss. It will be more accurate assessment of human success. Ecocriticism draws the attention of the world to the crucial issues of environmental degradation through the forum of literature. Nature and culture are inclusive terms.

Ecocriticism is committed to make the world less unjust. Well-conceived and sincerely implemented policies can make difference to people. High economic growth rates do not at all mean inclusive growth. The present policies in India are ill equipped to correct chronic poverty.

Policies and institutions are central to a country's ability. The nation is fed up with corruption. A human society based on inequality decays in the course of time. It aims at creating the harmonious relationship between Nature and human nature. It is against the exploitative development. The ecological analysis of the human life reflected in literature has been called ecological Criticism or Ecocriticism. The critical theory deals with the relationship between the human life and the nature. It transcends the exclusive categories of centre and periphery. It is the high time now to ponder over the evil consequences of industrialization and mechanization, globalization, privatization, and liberalization. It is the study of the interrelationship between nature and human life.

The environment nurtures, uplifts our senses and sustains our existence. Wendell Berry explores the political and moral implications of degrading and neglecting place in the novels such as *The Memory of Old Jack* (1976). In the United States the environmental literature includes poetry, fiction, and drama that scrutinize the relationship between humans and the natural environment.

The consciousness of the ethical component of literature is an important principle of the new ecological literary criticism or ecocriticism. The writers such as Berry Lopez, Terry Tempest Williams, Rick Bass, Robert Michael Pyle, Scott Russell Sanders, Wendell Barry, Gary Snyder and other environmental writers achieve not only aesthetic brilliance but also an understanding of human society's relationship with the planet.

Literary artists consider that values are at the heart of their work. Literary scholars give the utmost importance to the issues of human values and attitudes. Environmental writers create interest among their readers. They present a long-term vision of our relationship with the planet. They stimulate ethical reformation.

We have approached the 21st century. It has become clear that the model of free economy, Liberalization, Privatization and Globalization does not work. The problems of environmental degradation, poverty and domestic inequality have begun to threaten the very existence of the society and nation. They are threatening the quality of human life and security of nation. The model has proved ultimately self-defeating, as it threatens the beneficiaries of the so called progress. The world needs an alternative approach. The new approach is of Sustainable Development. The development pattern should create social cohesion rather than social inequality.

The development pattern should aim at the improvement of the quality of life. Environmental degradations affect the quality of life. In absence of healthy environment people are victimized by various types of diseases. Future generations feel insecure. Economic development pattern is responsible for the present problems. The problems are endemic not incidental. We need to reassess what we mean by economic and social progress. We should introduce fundamental changes in the economic and social development to achieve genuine development.

Poverty is the mother of all ills. Poverty is responsible for the rise in crimes, anti-social behaviour. The shadows of globalization and deregulation of markets have made even middle class vulnerable and insecure. Unequal society cannot stand the challenges, it breaks down. The middle class instead of solving the problem of the decay of the society want to evade the responsibility. They try to find peace and security within the four walls of their home. The people confront fear and tension and anxiety in their homes too. The sustainable development is the best model of development which improves the standard of life for all. The market economy has belittled the governments in the various countries of the world. It has caused anarchy in some African countries like Nigeria.

In the present model of market economy people have developed distrust over the political institution which governs them. Democracy needs to be strengthened in the real manner. Deregulated Market mechanisms are responsible for the breaking down of the traditional cultural values. People are feeling the loss of a sense of a community. The market economy has proved self-defeating. The supporters of market economy had claimed that it will solve all the problems. But instead of solving the problems it has generated severe problems before the society which are the threatening the very existence of society. The present model of development has given rise to violence and alienation among the people. Equality and inclusiveness strengthen the community. It creates the bond between individuals and the society. The society at large is united in the true sense.

The supporters of globalization said that the path of globalization will reduce poverty but globalization actually widened the gulf between the rich and the poor. We need a new direction of development. The new direction of such a type which will not give rise to division in the society but it will create cohesion in the society. Conventional economic and social policies are creating the problems instead of solving them. The quality of life is declining: The problems of availability of drinking water, homes, jobs, security have become severe. There is the rise in crimes all over the world. The poverty and inequality within the society has been threatening the very security of the nations. The people have developed disaffection for the politicians and the politics as an institution. Because politicians have become very selfish, they do not have commitment for the inclusive development. They have made the business of politics for their own selfish interest. Ecocriticism addresses these interlocking problems. The Real World offers the vision for the twenty-first century which is appropriate for every nation and every century:

> Our vision is of a Britain in which a reduction in inequality and an increase in both collective and individual security provides everyone with the opportunity to fulfill their potential, in which greater social cohesion strengthens both national and local communities; in which cultural diversity is celebrated; in which the improved provision of social goods raises everybody's quality of life even as material consumption falls to sustainable levels; in which a thriving democracy allows all to participate. (*The Politics of the Real World*, p. 125)[6]

Ecocriticism is avowedly political mode of analysis. It enables us to analyze and criticize the world in which we live. Culture is something lived, part and parcel of one's everyday existence. The authentic culture must be natural.

Radical changes have taken place in the study of literature during the last decades of the twentieth century. The human beings themselves have done a lot of damage to the nature and ultimately to themselves. The harmony of humanity and nature enhances the quality and standard of life. It is closely related to history, philosophy, psychology, art history, and ethics. It is a political mode of analysis of literature, as the comparison with feminism and Marxism suggests. It draws much from the environmentally oriented developments in philosophy and political theory. It sees a synthesis of environmental and social concerns. The theory is moral and political oriented.

John Passmore has made a distinction between 'problems in ecology' and 'ecological problems'. According to him problems in ecology are scientific problems which need hypothesis, experiment they need scientific analysis but ecological problems have arisen out of our dealing with nature. Ecocriticism helps to define, explore and resolve ecological problems and other consequent problems. Structuralism and post-structuralism dealt with the linguistic function of the signs that relate to each other. They do not refer to the real things, events and incidents on the earth.

It is an interdisciplinary approach that draws on literary and cultural theory, philosophy, sociology, psychology and environmental history and ecology. It has profound moral and political significance in 21st century.

Ecocriticism is the study of the relationship of the human and the non-human. It analyses the human life in the context of nature. Ecocriticism supports indigenous ways of life as potential models for a harmonious existence on the earth. It explores human life in the scenario of globalization, privatization and liberalization. Environmental crisis poses severe threats to the values, political, economic and cultural life of the people in various nations of the world.

Ecocriticism began in the 1990s. It has historical background. From ancient times various people have been expressing concerns about the natural world. Ecocriticism takes a strong ethical stand. It has a commitment to the natural world as an important thing rather than as an object of study only. It is the very young school of Literary Criticism or Movement. It explores how to use the stored energy of literature into effective political action for solving the contemporary problems. Lawrence Buell published *The Environmental Imagination*, where he defines "Ecocriticism as a study of the relationship between literature and the environment conduced in the spirit of commitment to natural environment." It explores environmental issues and its influence on the human life. It takes an ethical stand for effective change in the world. Ecocriticism is not only a critical approach to analyze literature but also a movement towards a sustainable development on the earth. It expresses the need for a cultural change in the world. It broadens the view of life to include non-human life forms and the environment as a part of the global community. Glotfelty rightly said that traditional criticism failed to address "green" issues. It is an important literary theory.

Evolution of Ecocriticism in Literary Studies

William Rueckert is the first person to use the term Ecocriticism. In 1978, Rueckert published an essay titled "Literature and Ecology: An Experiment in Ecocriticism". He made an important suggestion to apply ecology and ecological concepts to the study of literature. Ecologically minded individuals and scholars have been publishing progressive works of ecocriticism since the explosion of environmentalism in the late 1960s and 1970s. However, there was no organized movement or school to study the environmental aspect of literature. They were scattered and categorized under different subject headings: Pastoralism, Human Ecology, Regionalism, American Studies, etc.

British Marxist critic, Raymond Williams wrote a seminal critique of pastoral literature in 1973, *The Country and the City.* He professed decidedly a Green Socialism. Another early ecocritical text is Joseph Meeker's *The Comedy of Survival* published in 1974. He made an argument that environmental crisis is caused primarily by a cultural tradition in West of separation of Nature from Culture. The argument dominates Ecocriticism and Environmental philosophy. Ecocriticism analyses representation of nature in literary genres. Early efforts made by the critics were disunited. Ecocriticism crystallized into a coherent and organized movement in 1990s in the United States of America. In the mid-1980s, scholars began to work collectively to establish Ecocriticism as a genre. In 1990, at the University of Nevada, in Reno, Glotfelty became the first person to hold an academic position as a professor of Literature and the Environment. Association for the Study of Literature and Environment has burgeoned into an organization with thousands of members in the US alone. From the late 1990s, new branches of ASLE and affiliated organizations have been working in the United Kingdom, Japan, Australia, New Zealand, India, Taiwan, Canada, and Europe.

Ecocriticism: Definitions

Ecocriticism is an avowedly political and ecological form of criticism. It has moral and philosophical aim. Ecocriticism has borrowed methodologies and theoretical approaches liberally from other fields of literary, social, and scientific study.

Glotfelty defined Ecocriticism in *The Ecocriticism Reader: Landmarks in Literary Ecology*: "Ecocriticism is the study of the relationship between literature and the physical environment"[7] (*The Ecocriticism Reader,* p. xviii). Glotfelty has expressed the view genre of nature writing should be given dignity and value.

Ancient Classical Critics

Literary theory emerged in ancient Greece. When ideas were conceptualized, it gave birth to criticism as well as Greek philosophy. Plato's (428-347 BC) works signify the earliest example of literary criticism. In his *Dialogues,* Socrates represents the spirit of criticism. He opposes ignorance.

We must aim at the creation of the Green Economy and sustainable development. Environmental damage has long range consequences on the health and the economy of the country. There are limits to the resources available to us on the earth for development on the earth.

General Systems Theory focuses on the links and interactions between the elements that comprise the entirety of the system. Ecology explores the relationship between organisms and environment within the ecosystem as a whole. Environment supports all lives on the earth. When one element of a system changes, it brings about wide effects in the system.

Globalization is essentially a Post-World War II phenomenon. Development plans and projects should not threaten the cultural heritage. Knowledge and land are intimately bound to one another is a belief widely shared among indigenous peoples. They also believe that the natural world is alive, spiritually replete:

> We are indigenous people to this land...our brothers are all the natural world...remember that as long as (we) exist, so will you. But when we are gone, you too will go. (Oren Lyons, quoted in Dooling and Smith, 1989, p. 274)[8]

Human and non-human interpenetrate. Affiliational ties between the human and the non-human are crucial. Nature has sustained the lives of the people for hundreds of years. We cannot escape the fact of interdependency. April Bright rightly said:

> It is part of our responsibility (to be) looking after our country. If you don't look after country, country won't look after you. (p. 59)[9]

By observing proper ceremonies people Protect the land and environment with responsibility. Natural world secures for its people health, balance, and survival. Maori lawyer Moana Jackson remarks about the responsibility of the environment:

> The traditional Maori law defined the ancestral responsibility to maintain order and protect the land by ensuring a balance between the interlined animal, plant, spirit and human worlds. (1988, p. 40)[10]

To treat something with respect involves knowledge. Knowledge plays an integral role in sustaining the natural order.

In the 1960s people started to recognize the gravity of environmental pollution. People's attitude to nature decides what they do to the environment. Exploitation of the environment has been ruthless. We should reject the view that nature has no reason to exist except to serve humanity.

Human Treatment of the Environment in Hinduism

Hindu religion emphasized the human treatment of the environment. It has taught harmony with and respect for nature. It influenced other religions such as Jainism and Buddhism. It has been in recent times unable to sustain a caring attitude towards nature. It strengthens human respect for God's creation.

The seers of the Vedic period explored the relationship between human beings and nature. It is incomparable to any other religious and cultural traditions. They acknowledged Five Great Elements Earth, Air, Space, Water, and Light. The Upanishads make a true assessment of the origin, the nature, and the destiny the human beings and of the universe. These five Mahabhutas are cosmic elements which create, nurture, and sustain all forms of life. Water brings health and peace to the people.

The Prithvi Sukta

The Atharva Veda (about 2000 BCE) contains 63 verses devoted to Devi Vasundhara, the Goddess Earth evoking her benevolence. It exemplifies the relevance of environmental sustenance, agriculture, and biodiversity to human beings. It mentions that the preservation of the original fragrance of earth is essential so that its natural legacy is sustained for future generations.

The Prithvi Sukta also mentions a very important and relevant idea in all times that is cities should be planned in such a way that the land remains a place of worthwhile living for all, with its natural beauty preserved.

It is the responsibility of all human beings to protect, preserve and care for the environment. There is a deep bond between the earth and human beings as envisioned in Atharva Veda, book XII, hymn I, Verse 16. A comprehensive ecospirituality is reflected in Hinduism which is not found in any other religious traditions.

Human greed and exploitative tendencies have been the main causes of the environmental destruction. Inter religious and inter cultural conflicts and wars have also contributed to the environmental problems. Instead of exploiting nature, man should live in harmony with nature. In *Yajurveda*, it is mentioned that all lives, human and non-human are of equal value and all have the same right to existence. The Buddhist emperor, Ashoka (273-236 BCE) expressed his concern about the welfare of creatures, plants, and trees through pillar edicts at various places. He prescribed various punishments for the killing of animals. Pure water has the healing properties and medicinal value. The great epic *Mahabharata* states that pollution causes diseases of the mind and body too and both are inter-connected.

The concept of *Vasudhaiva Kutumbakam* exemplifies the entire universe as a single family. All living and non-living beings are considered the members of the extended household of Devi Vasundhara. The concept of *Vasudhaiva Kutumbakam* encourages cooperation between every creature on the planet earth. For ancient Hindus, both God and nature were to be one and the same. Ethical beliefs and religious values influence people's behaviour towards others.

> Let us not forget that all religions and cultures will be judged by future generations by the depth of their response to the problems generated by our rape of the planet. Any religion or culture which refuses to respond to this challenge will be judged for its silence. Because in the final analysis, the environmental crisis that we are facing today is not only a crisis of science and technology, nor a crisis of human values alone, but also a crisis of human spirit. (Dwivedi, O.P., *Classical India,* p. 48)[11]

Spirituality and ethics shape our attitude towards nature. Sustainable development includes spiritual and material uplift of all without exploitation and destruction. Spiritual understanding and cooperation at the global level are necessary for the realization of the welfare and caring of all. Eco-spirituality strengthens respect for nature. It influences and promotes sustainable development.

Spiritual understanding and cooperation at the global level will ensure the welfare and caring of all living and non-living beings on the earth. Sustainable development encompasses the spiritual and material upliftment of all without exploitation and destruction of others. India is a unique nation endowed with a rich Vedic-Hindu heritage of ecospirituality. The forces of materialism, consumerism, individual and corporate greed, the race of industrialization, capriciousness and corruption among politicians, bureaucrats are damaging the environment in India and elsewhere. All religions and cultures will be judged by future generations by the depth of their response to the environment. There is a blind belief in many nations of the world to advance economic growth at all costs. Economic growth has led to greed, poverty, inequality, injustice and environmental destruction.

The *Prithvi Sukta* maintains that attributes of earth such as purity, firmness and fertility are for everyone. No one group or nation has special authority over them. People should strive for the welfare of all and hatred towards none. Natural legacy of the earth must be sustained for the future generations. Lord Krishna celebrated importance of plants and vegetation in *Bhagavad Gita*. The Lord says that among all plants and trees, He is an Ashvattha tree—a tree which grows anywhere, even on a very hard surface (*Bhagavad Gita,* chapter 10, verse 26). The *Prithvi Sukta* also mentions that urban centers should be planned in such a way that the land remains a place for worthwhile living for all, with its natural beauty preserved. The Earth is considered as the main source of energy after the sun. The same energy is present in all living beings. Human greed and exploitative tendencies have been the main cause of environmental destruction.

Mother Earth has blessed us with all kinds of nourishment and serenity. The entire set of 63 verses of the *Prithvi Sukta* has been dedicated to Mother Earth. The *Prithvi Sukta* is the foremost ancient spiritual text from India. In it, it is said, "O Mother Earth! you are the world for us and we are your children; let us speak in one accord, let us come together so that we live in peace and harmony with all" (Atharva Veda, Book XII, Hymn I, verse 16).

These sentiments represent the deep bond between the earth and human beings, and show the true relationship between the earth and all living beings, as well as between humans and other life forms. Such a complete exposition of eco-spirituality is not found in any other religious tradition.

For ancient Hindus, both God and nature were to be one and the same. Human beings have no special privilege or authority over other creatures. They have a responsibility and obligations to other creatures. Hindus consider water to be a powerful medium for purification and also a source of energy. The healing properties and medicinal value of water has been universally acknowledged, provided it is pure and free from all pollution. The great epic, *Mahabharata*, states on pollution in general:

> From pollution two types of diseases occur in human beings. The first which is related with body and the other with mind, and both are interconnected. One follows the other and none exists without the other. (*The Mahabharata*, Rajdharma Anushasan Parv, and chapter 16, verses 8-9)[12]

Eco-spirituality entails that the entire universe is seen as an extended family, with all living beings in this universe as members of the household. This concept is also known as *vasudhaiva kutumbakam*, refers to all human beings as well as other creatures living on earth as members of the same extended family. We should develop the necessary maturity and respect for all other living beings.

Ethical beliefs and religious values persuade people's behaviour toward other including their relationship with all creatures and plants. Alien culture and values influenced India. The dangerous forces of materialism, consumerism, individual and corporate greed, the blind race to industrialize the nation immediately after achieving independence, and untrustworthiness as well as corruption among politicians, bureaucrats, and forest contractors have damaged India's environment.

Eco-spirituality can provide the values necessary for an environmentally caring world. It will not advance a blind belief in economic growth at all costs, creating in its wake greed, poverty, inequality, and injustice as well as environmental destruction.

Classical China

The Xunzi approach insists on the relatively separate spheres of actions of each of the three agencies heaven, earth and man. It establishes a connection between the three agencies. It emphasizes the significance of human effort and action. Psychologically it empowers human beings for socio-political activity. The tripartite relationship emphasises that human beings should model themselves after *tian* and *di*. Human beings are capable of manifesting humanity and rightness. These are two distinctly Confucian values. These special capacities are an endowment from *tian*. Compared with the humanism of Confucian thought, Daoist thought is much more inclusive.

In the *Laozi* and *Zhuangi*, a perspective favouring the human is ridiculed, seen as morally reprehensible. The *Laozi* rejects anthropocentric institutions and structures as transient artifacts of civilisation.

Daoist philosophy provides the basis for an aesthetic structure of the world. Human beings are merely parts of the permanent enduring, holistic reality. According to Daoist philosophy all forms of existence are connected. The reality is holistically comprised by the continuous communication of all forms of being. Daoist philosophy calls to human beings to observe and follow the ways of nature. It concerns with the equality of all forms of being.

Environmental Philosophy in Jainism and Buddhism

Jainism and Buddhism, religious traditions sprang in ancient India. Jainism is the older of the two. Rishabhanatha is the legendary founder of Jainism. The 24 great teachers (*Tirthankaras*) have urged their followers to live a life of simplicity, non-violence, vegetarianism. The great teachers preached a profoundly ecological lifestyle. Acharya Mahapragya believed that Environment protection is the human protection, polluting the environment is actually endangering the human life; man is the integral part of the ecosystem. "All life is bound together by mutual support and interdependence" (Tattvartha Sutra).

Ecocritical Theory emphasizes that economic policies should be environment friendly. The society should conserve the resources rather than their exploitation and waste.

Mahayana School of Buddhism gave importance to both nature and animals. People are enlightened in company of nature. Buddhism expressed concern for nature. Human beings' very existence is dependent on the environment. Instead of embracing the western development models blindly, there is the urgent need to cultivate a greater sensitivity to the ecosystem.

Ecocriticism is the newest school in Literary Criticism. Ecocriticism is the study of the relationship between nature and human nature. Literature and art influence human life.

Human life too influences the art and literature. It aims at creating the harmonious relationship between nature and human nature. It is against the exploitative development. The ecological analysis of the human life reflected in literature has been called Ecological Criticism or Ecocriticism. The critical theory deals with the relationship between the human life and the nature. It transcends the exclusive categories of centre and periphery. It is the high time now to ponder over the evil consequences of industrialization and mechanization, globalization, privatization, and liberalization. It is the study of the interrelationship between nature and human life.

To get a complete view of human life, we must think class, race, gender and nature together. Ecocriticism expresses a deep concern for the harmonious relationship between human life and nature. Henry David Thoreau's life at Walden was a beautiful example of simple living and high thinking. He explained why he went to live there:

> I went to the woods because I wished to live deliberately, confront only the essential facts of life, and see if I could not learn what it had to teach, and not, when I came to die, discover that I had not lived. (Thoreau, *Walden*, p. 1)[13]

Literature and art have always shown deep attachment with nature. All works of fiction take place in an environment that is setting. Environment impacts characters, action on to subsequent generations that is valuable.

Ecocriticism is against the exploitative kind of development. It appeals to the people to stop the life of self-destruction. Development at the cost of nature is no development at all. In almost all religions the reverence has been attributed to all life forms. The concepts like race, class and ideology have all altered the ways of our understanding the present. We cannot neglect the idea of nature in the present time. Our understanding of nature makes what we are. Ecological value is the significant part of our value system. To understand the predicament of the human beings and immense possibilities ahead, we must think class, race, gender along with nature.

Ecocriticism has at its centre the quality of human life. It substantially focuses on the health of the ecosystem. To protect the people from becoming environmental victims is clearly a task of the first order of importance in the world today. It links concerns of social justice to concerns of environmental quality. Environmental problems are inseparable from other social, economic, and cultural problems. Because environment affects every aspect of people's lives, their economic, political social and ritual are all affected by it. The very culture of the people has been affected by the environment. The life and culture of the people are interlinked with the land. The human community has experienced both environmental and cultural degradation. The former is seen, the latter is unseen. Togetherness in the community is a necessary condition of survival.

Due to dissociation of human life from nature, people lost the meaning of life. Many things are responsible for the environmental degradation in developed and developing countries. Respect is cognitive as well as moral virtue. To treat something with respect involves knowledge—it plays an important role in sustaining the natural order.

Environmental Security

Environmental security is inextricably linked to development. Poverty and environmental destruction go hand in hand. People need clean water, fertile land, and fuelwood resources for their daily survival. The life and culture of the people is intertwined with the land. Destruction of the land and environment creates havoc in economy, culture, and lives of the people.

The Classical Greek Tradition

Ancient Greek thinkers believed that whatever stance we adopt towards nature and the universe bound to affect the way we live. Human beings are not isolated items, cut off from the world. We are parts of a wider whole, which is governed by the same principles that should govern human life. We should exhibit moderation towards nature rather than arrogance. We should not be enclosed in our private thought. We should be aware of wider surrounding. People should be awake. We should bring our mind in tune with the operations of the universe, which is common to all.

Socrates (ca. 469-399 BCE) was mainly interested in ethics. With Heraclitus, he is interested in self-knowledge. According to him, modest human wisdom consists in self-awareness. Self-awareness furthers a state by which one's mind can get rid of false beliefs. Harmony favours friendship with others in a harmonious society.

In Plato's view, no one is intrinsically superior to animals merely by being human. It is reason that matters. The universe has priority over its parts, including both humans and plants. Nature is the source of life.

The Laws equally emphasizes that "the land [chora] is our ancestral home, of which we must take greater care than children do of their mother, since it is a god and the mistress of mortal beings" (V 740a, 5-7).[14] Plato shows awareness of environmental problems, such as the deforestation of Attica and the increasing non-absorption by the soil of rainfall there. He criticizes a society full of ships but devoid of virtue. In his book, the *Critias,* Plato contrasts the situation of his contemporary Athens with the ideal environmental conditions of a past Athens which also excelled in virtue. He encourages human concern about the environment.

Aristotle believed that there is some kinship between humans and animals. He appreciated surrounding natural environment. He said that human beings should not be hostile to the environment. He urged us to respect nature. He articulated the view that human art can improve on nature (Phys. II 8, 199a, 15-16). He felt the need to establish an ethical system, which should spell out the goals for which humans should strive. Humans can improve the state of the world in which they are parts. Overall good of the world itself is superior to the interests of people. The good of a city is superior to that of an individual. Aristotle said in *Politics* "For the whole is necessarily prior to the parts": without the whole, the parts lose their proper function (Pol. I 1, 125a 20-22).[15] He supported a life of moderation as opposed to excess in all levels, including a greed for sensual pleasures, power or money. He emphasized the divine kinship between the highest in humans and the cosmos.

The Stoics (fourth century BCE to second century CE) advocated a life in harmony with nature. We should follow a holistic rather than an individualistic perspective to obtain happiness. The whole is superior to the parts, even if there is the hierarchy between the species.

Many Platonic ideas are revived in the philosophy of the Neoplatonist Philosopher, Plotinus (ca. CE 205-70) and his successor Porphyry (ca. CE 205-70). Plotinus encourages us to raise ourselves from the level of dispersion and multiplicity in which our several individual egos are buried. He asked us to discover a level of unity and communication with the whole of nature which promotes sympathy toward all of its aspects and creatures. Higher levels of self-awareness reveal, the self is not diminished, but increased by attaining union and identity with the whole of nature and the universe. Porphyry emphasizes that we should treat earth as our mother and nurse. Philosophers have made valuable suggestions to integrate human life into the broader environment. The ancient Greek and Hellenic philosophers tended not to dissociate their own lives from a wider world view. Self-knowledge is concerned with what exactly our place in the larger world is.

Human beings have basically two choices; one is enclosed in private thoughts and interests and the other is to bring mind in harmony with nature. True wisdom lies in living in harmony with nature. We should try to preserve cosmic harmony through our behaviour. We discover ourselves as part of nature. Modest human wisdom consists in self-awareness. One's mind should get rid of false beliefs.

Mutual aid is the basis on which sustainable human societies can be built. According to Muir value of wild nature consists in two features: one was its beauty, from his perspective as a theist, it was a way of experiencing the divine. Leopold recognized that nature is the source food, minerals, and sport for human beings. Leopold urged farmers and foresters to avoid merely utility based ways of thinking about the nature.

He said: "A thing is right when it tends to promote the integrity, beauty and stability of the land; it is wrong when it tends otherwise."

Environmental Perspectives in Classical China

Confucianists in China had an essentially humanistic focus. Confucianism emphasized the significance of human effort and action and to empower human beings for socio-political activity. Chinese people held the view that cooperation between tian – God, di – earth and ren – man is considered very essential. The wellbeing of the universe depended on the successful cooperation between of three forces in their respective fields.

Ecospiritualism in Classical India

People's attitude to nature is decisive in their behaviour towards nature. The seers of the Vedic period perceived the subtle relationship between human beings and nature. The Vedic Seers acknowledged that Five Great Elements Earth, Air, Space, Water, Fire (The Panch Mahabhutas—Prithvi, Vayu, Akash, Apah, Agni) are cosmic elements which create, nurture and sustain all forms of life.

The Prithvi Sukta

The Prithvi Sukta comprises 63 verses have been dedicated to Mother Earth. It is the foremost ancient spiritual text from India which enjoins all human beings to protect, preserve and care for the environment. Hindu scriptures preach the people to seek peace and live in harmony with nature. The Prithvi Sukta maintained that Nature in its pristine beauty and health enhances the quality of human and non-human life in both rural as well as urban centre of habitat. It expresses an important concern about the planning of cities. It mentioned that cities should be planned in such a way that natural beauty of the land is preserved and it remains a place of worthwhile living for all. It appeals People to come together, live in peace and harmony. Cordiality and graciousness in relationship with other human beings will ensure environmental protection which entails their own survival and protection. Stronger connections are made between the issues of social justice and the environment.

By 1993, ecological literary school emerged as a new school in literary criticism. Fragmented, compartmentalized and over specialized way of knowing the world is one of the crucial reasons for environmental degradation.

The Classical Greek Environmental Philosophy

The classical Greek philosophers held the view that our attitude to nature and the universe is a determining factor which decides our way of life. They thought that animals and humans are not different in any significant way. Both of them have the equal possibilities of rise and fall. The development of inherent capacities and abilities elevate their life. According to Plato no one is intrinsically superior to animals by merely by being human. It is reason and feeling that matter. In his famous book *The Statesman,* Plato said that division between the humans and animals is unnatural. Nature is the source of life. In the *Critias,* Plato expressed the view that the society with the ideal environmental conditions excel in virtue. Plato contrasts the situation of his contemporary Athens with the ideal environmental conditions of a past Athens which also excelled in virtue. A life in harmony with nature is the rational way of life. Aristotle advocated a life of moderation rather than excesses. Eco clubs have been established. Ecocriticism fosters the basis for a natural and healthy relationship between human beings and the earth. Feelings establish the link between our intellect and the physical world. The ecological blindness in the society must be remedied to enhance the standard of the culture. Nature has intrinsic moral and aesthetic value. Nature limits excessive air pollution. Nature is aesthetically valuable. We should appreciate nature holistically and interactively.

Judaism and the View of Nature

Judaism has a rich and composite tradition regarding human communication with the natural world. There is no one distinct Jewish view of nature. Judaism proposes a radical anthropocentrism. Nature is viewed merely as a resource for the satisfaction of human interests, wants, and needs. Jews of Europe have lacked a direct relationship with nature for 500 years. Majority of the Jews have settled in cities for the sake of business. To be Jewish is to live in a human community, devoted to the establishment of human institutions, the study of the Torah, and the worship of God. Torah is the revealed word of God. Judaism clearly confines the human dominion, ownership, and freedom of action within the natural world. The humanity has the power to use natural resources, but there are clearly limitations on human freedom regarding the natural world. Authority does not mean unrestricted domination. Natural world is an expression of God's creation. The Torah and nature both are the expressions of the divine in the world. Fundamental Jewish tradition regards that humanity is the steward of the natural world, not its owner. Protection, preservation and care of Nature is a religious belief and a way of life in Judaism. Several commandments have expressed the concern that the general health and well-being of the human community depends on the quality of the natural world.

Jewish tradition holds the view that humanity does not own the natural world. Judaism is a theocentric religion. In Judaism the world belongs to God. God himself, not human life and welfare, is the source of religious and moral obligation. Humanity cannot have an unrestricted dominion over the natural world because the world belongs to God. Humanity is merely the divinely appointed guardian of the natural world which belongs to God.

Observance of Sabbath is connected to the notion of the stewardship. Humanity is the accountable guardian of God's creation. Judaism has expressed the principle that there should be balance of the economic, environmental and even religious development of the people. Open areas were preserved. There is also a right to quietness. Judaism is against the hybridization of plants and animals. Environmental regulations benefit the human community. There is a belief that human beings should not alter the God's creation. It has many principles which are directly related to the environmental philosophy. It prescribes the attitude of well-being of all living beings. Compassion for all living beings is a moral obligation in Judaism. "All creation is linked together in a bond of unity," which human beings should preserve (*The Torah*).

Judaism is concerned more with specific concrete commandments than with abstract ethical theories. There are many realistic commandments concerning human actions disturbing the natural world. Several commandments concern the general health and well-being of the human community as it is situated in the natural world. The preservation of open and undeveloped space was considered an important amenity for the human community. There is the mandate to establish a *migrash,* an open space one thousand cubits wide around all cities in Israel, in which agriculture and building would be prohibited. Open areas were preserved, and restrictions were placed on agriculture and other industries for the overall well-being of the human community situated in a particular environment. There are many laws that show concern for the quality of the environment in Jewish life. Judaism conceives that nature is the result of a divine plan. Human actions must not change God's plan of the creation. Hybridisation or the mingling of the species violates natural law, the principles of God's creation.

The preservation of species is one aspect of the maintenance of the divine plan that has enormous ramifications for contemporary environmental issues. There are clearly Jewish traditions and commandments to protect endangered species of animals. The laws concerning stewardship assure the overall quality of the human environment and the maintenance and sustainability of natural entities and species as part of God's creation.

In Jewish tradition a respect and reverence for life in all its forms is vital. It requires a concern for the well-being of all living beings—an attitude of universal compassion. The Jewish tradition recognises the divine presence in the entire world of creation. Compassion for all living beings is a moral obligation in Judaism. For the preservation of human life, it is necessary to protect nature. The *bal tashchit* is a religious and moral law that requires a contemplation of the social implications of actions that harm non-human entities. It concerns the proper human response to the non-human environment. Theocentric perspective of Judaism is the fundamental basis of the idea of stewardship. The world belongs to God. Human beings should not destroy the natural entities because such entities are the property of God. God's property cannot be destroyed for insignificant human purposes. *Bal tashchit* is not an anthropocentric principle at all. The principle is not designed to make life better for humanity; it is not meant to ensure a healthy and productive environment for human beings. It does not have the purpose to guarantee or promote human interests. The purpose of *bal tashchit* is to maintain respect for God's creation. It reaffirms God's ownership of the land.

Humanity should acknowledge the limits of human wisdom. We err when we believe that the events of the world must have a rational explanation relevant to human life. Theocentrism is the driving force of *bal tashchit*. Destruction is not an evil because it troubles human life—it is an evil because it harms the realm of God and His creation.

Nature is the expression of the creative power of God. Nature has an intrinsic value. Natural objects are valued, and cannot be destroyed, because they belong to God. They are sacred, not in themselves. God's creative process has made them sacred. Nature has an value independent of human interests. It is the expression of the creative power of God.

Human beings are the servants and stewards of God's creation. Gordis concludes that "Judaism insists that human beings have an obligation not only to conserve the world of nature, but to enhance it" (1990, p. 10). Natural world is the creation of God. She has a force, a presence that cannot be ignored. Nature is the realm in which humans interact with God.

E.L. Allen writes: "Nature is envisaged as one of the spheres in which God meets man personally and in which he is called upon to exercise responsibility" (Allen, 1951, p. 100). "The untamed world beyond the frontiers of human society is fraught with the numinous, it is a constant reminder that man is not master in the world but only a privileged and therefore responsible inhabitant of it" (Allen, 1951, p. 103). Judaism shows reverence for the natural world and God.

Christianity and the Natural World

Christianity upholds the independent value of natural creatures. It is committed to an ethic of responsible care and stewardship of the natural world. Central Christian teachings support ecological compassion. Belief in creation implies that the world does not belong to humanity but is God's world, full of God's glory. Jesus expressed the view that God is concerned with each and every human. Individual animals also have intrinsic value in the eyes of God. Humans and non-human animals are alike fellow creatures. Animals are not to be regarded as merely of instrumental value. Jesus has given parables about stewardship and accountability for the use of resources. Human body, however, has a beauty and dignity expressive of the glory and beauty of its creator (Bauckham, 1996, pp. 120-21). Francis Bacon (1561-1626) assumed an anthropocentric position. Rene Descartes (1596-1650) rejected the view that everything is made for humanity. Within his rationalist approach animals were regarded as machines. Plant life has its own intrinsic value. It upholds the independent value of Nature. Christian and secular ethics accept that it is wrong to treat non-human animals as simply means to human ends. Charles Darwin (1809-82) presented discovery of evolution by natural selection in *The Origin of Species* in 1859. He conveyed the continuity between humanity and other species. In *The Descent of Man* (1871), Darwin drew the implication that nature cannot be regarded as hierarchy, with humanity as a special creation at its apex, and other species existing for humanity's sake (Nash, 1989, pp. 42-45).

We should devise sustainable means of survival which preserve most remaining creatures and habitats, together with the system on which they and we depend. Wild creatures have the independent value. Christianity supports environmentally sensitive attitudes and policies. Theistic belief in creation can inspire sustainable relations between humanity and the rest of the natural world.

The Bible endorses the independent value of natural creatures and accepts a caring and respectable place for non-human nature. Stewardship is best construed as involving humble recognition of the intrinsic value of fellow creatures.

As human beings have intrinsic value, so animals too have intrinsic value. Neither the Old Testament nor the New Testament expresses the anthropocentric view of the world. Anthropocentricism has the view that nothing but humans and their interests are the most important things in the world. In the Bible Theocentricism is found. It expresses the belief that the world exists for the God's glory.

Genesis first implies some kind of superiority for humans over animals. It also has expressed that Humans and animals are like fellow-creatures. Animals are not to be treated that they have only the instrumental value, they exist for the sake of humans. Teachings of responsibility and compassion to non-humans pervade the Old and New Testament. The Biblical view is that Nature should not be just treated as resources for the well-being and development of human beings. Nature has its own independent intrinsic value.

Jesus through parables has emphasized that human beings should show consideration and compassion in their treatment of the non-humans. He urged to cherish and preserve the natural environment. Christianity appeals for environmentally sensitive attitudes and policies. Religious beliefs can inspire sustainable relations between humanity and the rest of the Nature.

Islam and Nature

The Qur'an is believed to be God's actual speech revealed in history. The Qur'an is the supreme guide for all its dimensions. The principles of Islam uphold the ecological values. Nature is the means through which God communicated to humanity. The physical world nourishes, supports, and sustains the process of life, in particular human life. Whole cosmos is an integral system. The Qur'an does not admit of a separation between the natural environment and the divine environment.

God has the dominion over the heaven and the earth. Human beings cannot arrogate to themselves absolute power and capricious control over nature. They must submit to the commands of the God. This is the core of the humanity's regency over the nature.

Human beings are part of nature. They are a natural entity. The Qur'an teaches that to damage, offend, or to destroy the balance of the natural environment is to damage, offend or destroy oneself. Any injury inflicted upon the other is self-injury. This is a central principle of Qur'anic ethics. Qur'an was a superbly rich literary document that contained broad and general principles. It has all manners of poetic variations and rhetoric embellishments. Its metaphors and imagery is highly evocative. Its expressions provide enormous possibilities for the imagination. The Qur'an is full of references to nature, natural forces, natural phenomena and natural beings. The Qur'an has the notion of unity of the God, environment and humanity in general.

The Qur'an reveals that the physical world existed to nourish, support and sustain the process of life. It does not permit people to get absolute power and capricious control over nature. The Qur'an speaks that humankind is thoroughly natural creation. It has 114 chapters, 31 of that are named after natural things and processes.

The natural world is a fully organized system. Human beings are the part of the natural system. They are a natural entity. They are an integral element of the overall ecological balance. The Qur'an comprises the moral principle that human beings should not offend or destroy nature, as in the destruction of nature lies the destruction of humanity. Humanity, God and Nature constitute a highly complex but coherent and integral system.

The Qur'an contains the issues of social and economic justice. It deals with the protection and preservation of nature and sustainable use of nature. It emphasizes the fundamental principle that world is not in existence for one generation of human beings. Human are not superior to other creatures in the nature but they are equal with other animals.

The Formalist Approach

Formalist literary criticism is a movement that concentrated on analyzing the internal structure of a literary text. Form is much more than sentence patterns. It is the relationship of stanzas in a poem. John Crowe Ransom wrote *The New Criticism* in 1941. The New Critics emphasized on form. A systematic and methodological formalist approach appeared in literary criticism with the rise of New Criticism in 1930s. The New Critics included John Crowe Ransom, Allen Tate, Robert Penn Warren, and Cleanth Brooks. They published an elegant literary magazine called *The Fugitive*. They viewed literature as an organic tradition. They emphasised the rigorous and analytical reading of literary texts. New Criticism became a dominant critical system by the 1950s.

The New Critics sought precision and structural tightness in the literary work. They called for an end to the matters outside the literary texts. New Critics excluded the reader's response, author's intention, historical and cultural contexts, and moralistic bias from their analysis. They believed that the structure and meaning of the text are intimately connected. New Criticism fell out of favour in 1970s, as poststructuralism, deconstructionist theory emerged and vied for the attention in literary studies. William K. Wimsatt and Monroe Beardsley published a classic and controversial New Critical essay entitled "The Intentional Fallacy." They argued strongly against the relevance of an author's intention in the analysis of a literary text. In another essay, "The Affective Fallacy," Wimsatt and Beardsley discounted the reader's personal response to literary work as a suitable means of analyzing a text. Reader Response Theorists repudiated the affective fallacy. Stanley Fish criticized Wimsatt and Beardsley in his essay "Literature in the Reader" (1970).

The New Criticism was popular through the Cold War years in America. It offered a relatively straightforward approach to teaching students how to read and understand poetry and fiction. Brooks and Warren published *Understanding Poetry* and *Understanding Fiction* which both became standard pedagogical textbooks in American high schools and colleges during the 1950s, 60s, and 70s. Formal elements such as rhyme, meter, setting, characterization, and plot were used to identify the theme of the text. The New Critics also looked for paradox, ambiguity, irony, and tension to establish the single and most unified interpretation of the text. The approach has been criticized as it constitutes a conservative attempt to isolate the text and to screen it from external, political concerns such as those of race, class, and gender. The New Criticism is no longer a dominant theoretical model in American Universities. However, some of its methods like close reading are still fundamental tools of literary criticism.

New Criticism is frequently seen as "uninterested in the human meaning, the social function and effect of literature." Terence Hawkes points out that the fundamental close reading technique is based on the Assumption.

The Psychological Approach

The Psychological Approach is a fascinating and rewarding critical approach. The mode of interpretation has enhanced understanding and appreciation of literature among the readers. No single approach can offer complete understanding of a literary text. Each critical approach has merits and demerits of its own. Psychological Criticism falls short in explanation of aesthetic qualities in the literary text. It has proved very useful in demystifying the thematic concerns and symbolism in the text. Psychological Approach is not a completely new approach in the twentieth century. Aristotle has made a very subtle use of it while setting forth his classic definition of tragedy. Sir Philip Sydney used it when he discussed about the moral effects of poetry. The Romantic poets as Coleridge, Wordsworth, and Shelley expressed psychological ideas in their theories of imagination.

During the twentieth century psychological criticism has come to be associated with Sigmund Freud and his followers. Jacques Lacan is the most significant of all his followers. Freud had a deep knowledge of, and love for literature. Psychological approach is a very important tool of critical analysis. The principles of Freudian Psychology have been used extensively in literary analysis.

Freud emphasizes on the unconscious aspects of human psyche. Freud has given convincing evidences in support of his theory. Most of the actions of the human beings are motivated by psychological forces. They have a very limited control over these forces. Freud made the observation that most of the individual's mental processes are unconscious. He made the second premise that all human behaviour is ultimately motivated by sexuality. According to Freud the primary psychic force is libido, or sexual energy. His disciples Carl Gustav Jung and Alfred Adler did not agree with him on this account.

According to Freud there are three psychic zones: the id, the ego, and the superego. He classified mental processes in three zones: the id, the ego, and the superego. The id is the reservoir of libido. It is characterized by a tremendous and amorphous vitality. It concerns with character. Psychoanalysis is a valuable tool in understanding literature and human nature. Freud believed that the most important principle for the organism is to attain the state of tranquility of the mind. An organism should master the emotions rather than being enslaved by those.

Feminism

Feminist literary criticism developed mostly since the beginning of the women's movement in late twentieth century. Simone de Beauvoir, Kate Millett, and Betty Friedan are the prominent theorists. According to them literary texts are models and agents of power. In her book *The Second Sex* (1949), Simone de Beauvoir has explained how a woman is constructed differently from men. Man constructs woman differently. Her writings have long lasting implications. Her idea that man defines the human, not woman is influential.

Feminism reflects concern with the silencing and marginalization of women in a patriarchal culture, a culture organized in the favour of men. Feminism is an overtly political approach.

Betty Friedan in her book *The Feminine Mystique* (1963) demystified the dominant image of happy American suburban housewife and mother. Women's organizations called for enforcement of equal rights and an end to sex discrimination. Millett's *Sexual Politics* (1979) is a very famous work in feminist literary criticism. It focused on the issues of gender and culture. Millett criticized capitalism, male power, crude sexuality, and violence against women. She argued that "interior colonization" of women by men is sturdy.

Elaine Showalter has identified three phases of modern women's literary development: the feminine phase (1840-80). The women writers imitated the dominant male traditions in this phase. The women advocated for their rights in the feminist phase (1880-1920). The female phase (1920-the present) is known for rediscovery of women's texts and women. Woolf's novel, *Mrs. Dalloway*, is the study of female subjectivity. Silence arises from the class, race or gender. Lack of education, economic struggles, and demands of nurturing silenced the women for centuries.

Cultural Materialism

Raymond Williams the British Neo-Marxist critic employed the term. A number of other critics and scholars of literature used the term to indicate the Marxist orientation of the New Historicism. They accepted Marx's view that cultural phenomena as a superstructure. It is determined by the material/economic base. Material forces and relations of production influence cultural and literary products profoundly in the historical era concerned. Cultural materialists comment on the political dimension of the literary text. They are committed to transform the society in which people are exploited on the basis of race, gender and class.

The New Historicist Critics analyse class dominance and exploitation in literary texts. They are committed to remake the present social order based upon inequality.

Reader Response Criticism

Reader Response Theory began as a reaction against New Criticism which dominated literary criticism for roughly half a century. Formalism misrepresents and oversimplifies a literary text. According to Formalist critics a literary text has its own existence. They do not observe any relationship between the text, and its creator, the historical time it depicts, or the historical period in which it was written. They find all meaning and value in a literary text.

Reader-response critics have taken a radically different approach to the study of literature. They feel that reader should not be ignored in the discussions of the reading processes. A text even does not exist, in a sense, until it is read by some reader. Reader-response criticism is not a monolithic critical position. They give important place to readers and their responses in interpreting a literary text. The following tenets reflect the main perspectives in the Reader-response position. The reader is the most important component in the process of literary interpretation. There is no text, unless there is a reader. The reader creates the text, as much as the author does. The process of reading is dynamic and sequential.

New Criticism

New Criticism appeared with its fetishistic notions of the utter autonomy of each single literary text. It viewed literature as a special kind of language which yields a special kind of knowledge. It was used as a pedagogical tool in the American classrooms. It did not require from students knowledge which is not strictly literary. For New Critics favorite text was the short lyric. Lyric could be detached from the larger body of texts with greater ease. Analysis of lyrics was fit for one hour in the undergraduate classroom. The most important problem arises out of New Critical practice is that it detaches literature from the crises and combats of real life. New Critics were the bourgeois gentlemen of the New South. They were the cultural heirs of the old slave owning class.

Northrop Frye attacked new criticism. He insisted that individual literary texts should be placed within wider, formalist narrative of all surrounding genres and literary modes. Literature and the critical approach must be concerned with the problems and opportunities in human life.

Poststructuralism: Deconstruction

Poststructuralism and deconstruction are practically synonymous. Deconstruction arises out of the structuralism of Roland Barthes. It is a reaction against the certainties of structuralism. Deconstruction identifies textual features like structuralism. Unlike structuralism it concentrates on the rhetorical rather than the grammatical. Texts are found to deconstruct themselves. They do not provide a stable identifiable meaning. Structuralism finds order and meaning in the text. Deconstruction finds disorder. The language constantly tends to refute its apparent meaning. Deconstruction finds that texts subversively undermine an apparent or surface meaning. It denies any final explication or statement of meaning. It questions the presence of any objective structure or content in a text. The practitioners of deconstruction celebrate the text's self-destruction. The text has the inevitable seed of its own internal contradiction. Deconstructionist held the view that text is always in a state of change. All texts are the open-ended constructs. There are indefinite numbers of meanings in a text; there is no ultimate meaning for the text. Jacques Derrida, the French philosopher has been the most important figure in deconstruction. According to Derrida, language is vital. Deconstruction has some shortcomings. Deconstruction is valuable, as some of its cautions are absorbed into other interpretive approaches.

Postcolonial Studies

Postcolonialism refers to historical phase undergone by third world countries after the decline of colonialism. Countries in Asia, Africa, Latin America and the Caribbean separated from European empires. They had to rebuild themselves. Bill Ashcroft and others edited *The Empire Writes Back* is a brilliant study of the postcolonial culture. Paul Gilroy has radically remapped cultural criticism in *The Black Atlantic*. Said criticises sharply the western conception of the East in the *Orientalism*. Frantz

Fanon, a French Caribbean Marxist, wrote about his horrific experiences in French Algeria. He deconstructed emerging national regimes that are based on inheritances from the imperial powers. He warned that class, not race, is a greater factor in worldwide oppression. New nations should not adopt the old patterns of colonial regimes. They should destroy the bourgeois inequalities from the past. Fanon's *The Wretched of the Earth* (1961) throws light on the decolonizing project of the third world countries.

Gayatri Chakravorty Spivak is among the most important figures in postcolonial feminism. She examines the effects of political independence upon subaltern in the Third World. She offers little hope for the subaltern woman's voice to rise up amidst the global social institutions that oppress her.

Cultural Studies

Cultural Studies arose from the social turmoil of 1960s. It examines interrelationships among race, gender, popular culture, the media, and literature. Cultural critics question historical and contemporary cultural conventions. Cultural Studies comprises elements of Marxism, Poststructuralism and postmodernism, feminism, gender studies, anthropology, sociology, race and ethnic studies, film theory, urban studies, public policy, popular culture studies, and postcolonial studies. Cultural critics concentrate on those social and cultural forces that either create community or cause division and alienation. Michel Foucault said that power is a whole of complex forces. It gives direction to the incidents and events.

Cultural Studies is politically engaged. Cultural critics oppose the power structures of society at large. They question inequalities within power structures. They seek to discover models for restructuring relationships among dominant and subaltern discourses. Culture constructs meaning and individual subjectivity. It relocates aesthetics and culture from the ideal realms of taste and sensibility.

Cultural Studies denies the separation of elite and popular culture. Today culture includes mass culture. Cultural studies analyses the cultural work. It also analyses the means of production. Literature is intimately connected with the concerns of our lives. It explores culture in relation to individual lives. Cultural critics attack social ills. A cultural study is referred to as "cultural materialism" in England.

Ecofeminist Literary Criticism

Ecological feminism or ecofeminism brings feminist insight to environmental philosophy. The Anthologies such as *Healing the Wounds: The Promise of Ecological Feminism* (Plant, 1989) and *Reweaving the World: The Emergence of Ecofeminism* (Diamond and Orenstein, 1990) began to appear in the late 1980s. Ecofeminists agree that there is a link between dominations of women and dominations of nature. The understanding of one is crucial to the understanding of the other. Ecofeminists argue that environmental critics should not neglect these important links. Merchant examines the emergence of modern science in Europe in the fifteenth to seventeenth centuries. She argues that the shift in world views from the organic to the mechanic was a major vehicle for the devaluation of both women and nature. There are connections between various types of oppression, domination, and exploitation. Adams argues that concern about animals is part of the ecological feminist project. Acknowledging their value is part dismantling the logic of domination.

Two-thirds of all African-Americans and Latinos in the United States reside in areas with unregulated toxic waste site. Toxic dumping is a problem concerning human well-being. It affects non-human as well.

Vandana Shiva's book *Staying Alive* (1989) is a classic. She has analysed development as a process, using India as an example. She has explained the negative impact of patriarchal style western development in India. Shiva argues that western-style progress creates poverty as it creates wealth. Shiva maintains that this kind of development destroys sustainable lifestyles and creates true material poverty for those who are developed.

The primary cause of species extinction is loss of habitat. Rapid climate change could be the ultimate destroyer of habitats. Climate change is harmful for human and other species too. Some locations that now have abundant rainfall will have inadequate rainfall. The problem of drinking water will be serious. Locations that now suffer drought may receive heavy rains. More people may perish from droughts and floods. Wars are fought over access to water for drinking, irrigation and manufacturing. Climate change is responsible for human illness and death.

Climate change prevents people from obtaining the necessary resources vital for their survival. Every human being needs some minimum amount of drinkable water and breathable air. We might construct an advanced industrial economy based on solar, wind and geothermal energy. Green House Gas emissions will be limited. Human beings on the planet need sound and sustainable economic development. Economy should make their life decent.

The aesthetic qualities of nature are commonly invoked to justify preservation of nature areas. The prominent reason is that nature is majestic, beautiful. Natural beauty constitutes an aesthetic good. Nature provides the basic human needs for the essentials of life. The appreciation of nature should be holistic and interactive. The natural environment is graceful, delicate, intense, unified and orderly. Nature is all beautiful in its own way. It is always aesthetically good. Carlson and others have developed a position called "positive aesthetics" John Ruskin held the view that the certainty of beauty was to be found only in nature.

Ecofeminism is an intellectual, activist, social, political and literary movement. It makes the critical connections between the domination of nature and the exploitation of women. It is a new way of seeing old problems of oppression and exploitation. Ecofeminists believe that environmentalism and feminism are intrinsically linked. Discrimination and oppression based on gender, race and class are directly related to the exploitation and destruction of the environment. Indian ecofeminist Dr.

Vandana Shiva has devoted her life to ending the industrial exploitation of Asia, South America and Africa.

French writer Francoise d'Eaubonne coined the term Ecofeminism *in* her book *Le Fe'minism ou la mort* (1974). She gives background and an explanation of her newly coined word ecofeminism. She observes that women have been reduced to the lower status by a male dominated society. Overpopulation is ruining both humanity and the earth. The earth is treated with the same disregard as women. Women must act to save themselves and the earth simultaneously. The two needs of saving earth and women are intimately linked. Women are important part of society in terms of number and significance of reproduction which should have given them a dominant position.

Francoise D'eaubonne discussed issues of ecofeminism in detail in her book, *Ecologie Feminisme: Revolution or Mutation*? Mutation or alteration through time—seems insufficient to effect what needs to be done urgently. Inattention to women's and earth's well-being have raised many problems. For solving these problems there is the necessity of a revolution in thought. Francoise D'eaubonne questioned the early nineteenth and twentieth century political movements—like socialism which failed to alter the state of things. The ecofeminist movement aims to allow history to continue rather our extinction from the earth as it happened with some animals and certain species of birds.

Ecofeminists argue for "human beings would finally be regarded as persons and not first and foremost as males or females. And our planet close to women become verdant again for everyone" (251). The extinction of people and planet is at stake. Only a revolution in thought and action can prevent extinction of human society and earth. The movement of ecofeminism effects a revolutionary change in mentalities and attitudes of the people. There is the need of moving beyond power politics and an equivalent necessity of less management of the land.

Challenges to Ecofeminist Philosophy

Certain critics of the ecofeminist movement have insisted that ecofeminism is an essentialist movement. Ecofeminists believe that women are closer to nature than men. They also believe that all living things are connected. Feminist and social ecologist Janet Biehl has criticized ecofeminism for focusing too much on a mystical connection between women and nature and not enough on the actual conditions of women. Deep ecologists have changed the anthropocentric view of nature. They have asked humans to think biocentrically. There is the necessity of moving beyond power politics. They appreciate the intrinsic value of everything in nature. We should follow a biocentric rather than an anthropocentric world view. It asks for an end to dualisms like male/female, thought/action, and spiritual/natural.

Ecofeminists around the world are working diligently to effect changes in attitudes toward women and nature. The changed attitude promotes the survival of all people, other living creatures and the earth. Ecofeminism is an important theory which gives us tools to assess the interconnections between women's oppression and the ecological crisis. They analyze global development's impact on women. According to sociologist Mary Mellor, Ecofeminists believe that gender analysis is critical in addressing environmental problems. Ecofeminists address issues like water pollution, deforestation, toxic waste dumping, agricultural development, sustainability, and animal rights and nuclear weapons policies. Ecofeminism is a global and multi-issued movement, with an ever growing community of activists and theorists.

Vandana Shiva is a physicist, author, activist, feminist and philosopher from India. She was a participant in the Chipko movement of the 1970s, which was a non-violent activism to protest and prevent deforestation in the Garhwal Himalayas of Uttarakhand, India then in Uttar Pradesh. Dr. Wangari Muta Maathai is best recognized for her development of the Green Belt Movement. She was the first African woman and the first environmentalist to win the Nobel Peace Prize (2004).

Ecofeminism is a social and political movement. It links environmentalism and feminism. Ecofeminists argue that a strong parallel exists between the oppression and subordination of women in families and society and the degradation of nature. The domination and exploitation of women, poor people and of nature is at the core of the ecofeminist analysis.

Ecofeminism or ecological feminism is a philosophy and movement which has united feminist and ecological thinking. It believes that the social mentality that leads to the domination and oppression of women is directly connected to the social mentality that leads to the abuse of the natural environment. Globalization for the sake of profit has given rise to many evils like destruction of nature and the injustice to women. The movement of ecofeminism addresses the problems of economic inequality, sustainability, environmental welfare, and animal rights on a global scale.

Political Dimensions of the Ecocriticism

The governments must take steps for decontamination of the environment in the affected areas and supply of pure drinking water. Inclusive growth cannot be achieved without removing corruption. The benefits of economic growth are not reaching all sections of society and there is need to address the gaps in the system for overall development. Corruption hurts inclusive growth.

The country's economic development should be more holistic to bring about sustained improvement in living standards. The people should easily access to education, healthcare and social security, among other things. Strengths of political system depend on the strengths of each individual member. Each individual must take personal responsibility for the deteriorating/maintaining global environment. True change is possible only when it begins inside the person. Mahatma Gandhi rightly said: "We must be the change we wish to see in the world." Climate change has tremendous effects on the political and social stability of civilization. The grand city of Fatepur Sikri was completely abandoned because of water shortage. Sudden change in the climate change deprived it water. Because of climate change many civilisations like Indus Valley civilisation, Mali civilisation collapsed.

David Orr, in *Earth in Mind* focuses not on problems in education, but on the problem of education. He argues what has gone wrong with the world, is the result of inadequate and misdirected education. He explains crisis we face, is one of mind, perception and values. He makes the contention that one of the goals of the liberal arts is to create a mood of sobriety without despair. He writes:

> This is a time of danger, anomie, suffering, crack on the streets, changing climate, war, hunger, homelessness, spreading toxics, garbage, barges plying the seven seas, desertification, poverty, and the permanent threat of Armageddon.... The often cited indifference and apathy of students is, I think, a reflection of the prior failure of educators and educational institutions to stand for anything beyond larger endowments and an orderly campus. The result is a growing gap between the real world and the academy, and between the attitudes and aptitudes of students and the needs of their time. (*Earth in Mind: On Education, Environment, and the Human Prospect* 2nd Revised Edition, p. 102)[16]

Rachel Carson wrote a classic book, *Silent Spring* about the threats of the environment. The environmental literature has a long-range impact. Destruction of the environment contributes to the regional and local problems. Deforestation wreaks havoc on the hydrological cycle. Eventually it causes a sharp decline in the amount of rainfall where the forests once grew. It results in migration of the people. Loss of nature contributes to the ecological tragedy of the country. Nature is a rich and complex resource. Hundreds of important medicines are derived from plants and animals. Future generation will face the problems in procuring the medical facilities if we continued with the same speed of destruction of nature incessantly.

The drive for economic welfare sacrifices public health and damages the environment. Communities have become aware about the role of corporations in undermining community welfare. Corporations have a little accountability for decisions that affect local communities. Many corporations have been following exploitative practices. People have expressed concern for the environment, jobs and economy related concerns. While raising current living standards, we should not undermine the environmental integrity of the future. The number of people fleeing from their homes has increased tremendously. People have been leaving their homes in search of natural resources such as water and fertile land. Economic growth is intimately linked with peace and security. Reconstruction of economy and strengthening natural resources are crucial for sustainable development.

The relationship between humans and nature is vital. The environmental pollution has been creating havoc on the earth. The Bhopal Gas Tragedy, Chernobyl catastrophe, to name a few, is grim manifestations of the emergent crisis of environmental destruction. We must reconfigure the ecological, political, and social.

The destruction of tropic rain forests will be catastrophic. Progress would not survive, without an ecological and environmental awareness. In human destruction of nature lies our own destruction. Howells and the humanists emphasized that Society should move in the direction of cooperation and unselfish behaviour. Ruthless and selfish social behaviour leads society towards destruction. Howell constructed a vision of what ought to be in Altrurian fiction. Altruism is the concept that would ideally direct the nation in its path of evolutionary progress. Howells utopia must be taken as an emblem of possibility, a goad towards reformist thinking, a catalyst for social change. Howell has a deep commitment for social reform. Planet's protective ozone layer is depleted. The critical loss of arable land and groundwater through desertification, contamination, and the spread of human settlement is a threat for human life. A tide of profit-and-growth driven globalization undermines sustainable development, our best hope for the future.

After 1980s markets have been deregulated. Public enterprises and services have been privatized. Increasing trust has been placed on private sector for the welfare services, for example, education, health, pension, etc. Large numbers of people have not got the benefits of the implementation of the new model of economic growth. The number of people living in absolute poverty has grown not declined. People are not feeling security in their jobs. The insecurity of employment has increased. We see the unequal growth in the world. There is the need of the introduction of the fundamental changes in the patterns of economic and social development. There is the rise in crime. Quality of life is getting worse rather than better because of the unequal development of the society.

Environmental problems have become severe. The greenhouse effect, depletion of the ozone layer and the loss of the biodiversity endanger the basic life support systems of the planet. Air pollution has been damaging children's health. The present model of economic development must be changed. The problems are not the symptoms of model's failure but of its success. Because of increasing inequality, large numbers of poor and unemployed people are excluded from mainstream society.

Human degradation of the environment is destroying the livelihoods and health of crores of people across the world. Rich are getting richer, while the poverty of the poor people is increasing. They are not able to fulfill their most basic needs. It is morally barbarous. Environmental degradation has been damaging the quality of life of rich and poor both. Air pollution, traffic congestion, loss of countryside, chemicalised food production methods encroach on everyday life. Crime and social disintegration corrode the lives of millions of low-income individuals. The dominant pattern of economic development is no longer generating net benefits but net costs. Therefore, change is essential. We need to re-examine the concept of economic and social progress. The future looks threatening, not hopeful.

We are losing the renewable resources—trees, soils, water. Nature enriches and enhances every culture. Nature ennobles the personal experience. Pollution and resource depletion cause damage to human health and quality of life. Natural environment provides essential resources and services for flourishing the human life. We should not reduce the capacity of the nature to provide necessary resources and services crucial to human life.

Water quality in river is declining. Rivers have become polluted. Urban air pollution has been making severe effects on the health of the residents of the cities. The loss of natural habitats and species has become a matter of great concern. Environmental improvement should be compatible with the economic progress.

Ecological system has difficulties adapting to rapid change. If CO_2 increase in the atmosphere, so does the temperature. The United Nations established the Intergovernmental Panel on Climate Change in 1989. The scientists expressed the strong opinion that the global warming is real, and the right time for action is now. Climate imbalance caused crop failures; it led to food riots in many countries of the Europe. The existing government fell in Europe. Crime epidemic surged in many countries. The number of suicides increased dramatically. Climate imbalance makes people desperate. 10,000 were killed in the initial eruption. 82,000 died of starvation in the following months in Indonesia.

Preservation of the environment is central to the future of the humanity. It has always been essential for the viability and success of any civilization. Environmentalists assert that we are, after all, the part of the earth. Unfortunately, dramatically our relationship with the earth changed since the industrial revolution. Health of the planet depends on the maintenance of complex balance of interrelated systems. Major climate changes may occur in a few decades.

The destruction of forests affects the hydrological cycle. In Ethiopia the forested land decreased from forty to one percent in the last four decades. The amount of the rainfall declined has declined very much, and the country has become a wasteland. The nation faced the prolonged drought. Famine, civil war, and economic turmoil caused a large amount of damage on the nation. Deforested regions face droughts.

The contamination of water resources worldwide is a strategic threat. We need instead to lasso our common sense. The rain brings us trees and flowers; the droughts bring gaping cracks in the world. The lakes and rivers sustain us; they flow through the veins of the earth and into our own. But we must take care to let them flow back out as pure as they came, not poison them without thought for the future (*Earth in the Balance* 114).

Effects of water pollution in Third World Countries are serious. The number of the victims of cholera, typhoid, dysentery, and diarrhea from viral and bacteriological sources has increased dramatically. Billions of people do not have an adequate supply of safe drinking water, proper sanitation. An average twenty-five thousand people die a day in third world countries because of the result of the diseases from contaminated water.

The health of the surface of the earth determines the health of the global environment. The forests play a crucial role in regulating the hydrological cycle. They stabilise and conserve the soil, recycle nutrients. They provide the most prolific habitats for living species. Many vulnerable species have become extinct due to the destruction of forests and wetlands. The destruction of the tropic rain forests is catastrophic. These are the most important sources of biological diversity. We should not destroy the integrity of the intricate web of life on the planet. Indigenous cultures depend on the forest. Ancient tribal societies are disappearing along with the destruction of the forests. They have managed their own environment successfully for thousands of years.

Hundreds of important medicines now in common use are derived from the plants and animals of the tropical forests. If we destroy all tropical rain forests, we will lose the richest storehouse of genetic information on the planet. We must protect the tropical rain forests for the medical needs of the future generations, as well as our own. Rain forests are the complex, rich and valuable resource for future generations. Deforestation causes a sharp decline in the amount of the rainfall. It causes loss of billions of topsoil each year. Deforestation has been responsible for migration. The millions of people migrated from Haiti to United States due to deforestation. Air pollution devastated European forests like Germany's beloved Black Forest.

Seriousness of the ecological issue is the indication of the depth of man's moral crisis. Man is organic with the world. His inner life moulds the world and is itself deeply affected by it. We must recover moral health and martial vigour. We should take stand for freedom.

We should not avoid our moral responsibility to posterity. Abraham Lincoln very aptly told our responsibility to future generations:

> Fellow citizens, we cannot escape history. We...will be remembered in spite of ourselves. No personal significance, or insignificance, can spare one or another of us. The fiery trial through which we pass will light us down in honour or dishonour, to the latest generations. We say we are for the Union. The world will not forget that we say this. We—even we here—hold the power and bear the responsibility. In giving freedom to the slave, we assure freedom to the free—honorable alike in what we give, and what we preserve. We shall nobly save, or meanly lose, the last best hope of earth. Other means may succeed; this could not fail. The way is plain, peaceful, generous which, just—a way which, if followed, the world will forever applaud and God must forever bless. (December 1, 1862 Message to Congress Lincoln)[17]

Towards an Alternative Model

Climate change exerts powerful effects on the political and social stability of civilisation. Widespread crop failures lead to food riots in every nation. Existing governments fell due to revolutionary fervor. Number of suicides increase dramatically in the areas which are affected by the inadequate rainfall. We should think strategically about our relationship with the earth. With personal commitment, change can be introduced in the larger civilisational systems. We should bring necessary changes in our thoughts and actions which are integral to our culture, for saving the earth. Albert Gore explained reasons for the degraded appreciation of the individual and nature:

> By definition, a wasted life is one that is seen as having no value in the context of human society. Similarly, if we see ourselves as separate from the earth, we find it easy to devalue the earth. The two issues—wasting lives and wasting the earth—are intimately connected, until we see that all life is precious, we will continue to degrade both the human community and the natural world. (*Earth in the Balance*, p. 162)[18]

In the 21st century, it has become clear that the model of economic and social progress which has dominated the second half of the twentieth century no longer works. The problems of environmental degradation, global poverty and domestic inequality devastate the gains which have been made. Security of nations and quality of human life is at risk. The current pattern of economic growth is ultimately self-defeating. Current patterns of growth have not solved the problems of environmental degradation, global poverty, inequality, unemployment, and quality of life in India or any other country. Current pattern of growth is actually the source of many problems. Growth does not create social cohesion. Growth in itself does not bring quality life. Current pattern of growth raises private incomes of a certain group of people. There is the need of availability of social good.

Security within and between nations depend on protection of the environment and eradication of poverty. Our development pattern should increase and distribute employment. Economic globalization has uprooted communities and destroyed settled cultures, in India, as throughout the world. Poverty follows from economic marginalization. The world needs an alternative growth pattern which fosters economic inclusion. Markets are essential but they must serve the interests of the society. Deregulated markets have reduced the role of national economies. National governments should possess the authority and power to influence and restrict market forces. Reforms in the institutions of politics and government are necessary for rejuvenation of democracy. Environmental degradation causes ill health. Environmental degradation has made the future of children bleak. Effects of poverty emerge in crime and anti-social behaviour. Globalization and deregulation of markets have made even middle-class jobs vulnerable. Unequal society generates tension and struggles. In an interdependent world there is no security behind protective walls. All should take the social responsibility. A society which upholds ethical principles is itself for many people a better place to live. A moral society cares for its less fortunate members. It takes care of natural environment, and for the idea of community.

Ecocriticism explores the possible ways to improve the lives of people who live in extreme poverty. Good economic policies have the power to change the lives of the poor people. Government has to take an important role to address the problems like inequality, unemployment, pollution. Government should be efficient and responsive.

The International Monetary Fund is a public institution. It was founded for maintaining economic stability through collective action at the global level. The United Nations had been founded on the belief that the collective action at the global level is necessary for political stability.

The IMF failed in its fundamental purpose of promoting global stability. The gap between the poor and the rich has been growing in both the developing and developed countries. Government should focus on providing essential public services. Growth should be more equitable and sustainable. Many government activities arise because markets have failed to provide essential services.

Privatization often destroys jobs rather than creating new jobs. Privatization has made matters worse in many countries. Russia provides a devastating example of the following the policy of privatization. It undermined confidence in democratic and market institutions. Social and political contexts cannot be ignored while pursuing the path of development. The greatest challenge is not in the institutions themselves but in mind-sets.

People should be careful of the environment. The decisions taken at the economic level should serve the interests of all not just a few. Karl Marx was aware of the adverse effects of capitalism on the workers. He provided an alternative model for development. Despite its flaws, Marx's model has had enormous influence in the developing countries. Billions of poor people expect that alternative model will serve their development needs. The collapse of the Soviet Union showed its weaknesses. The marked model dominated the world.

Deforestation continues, soil is eroded, water and air are poisoned, species are extinguished, human population and resource use are growing, and climate change caused by human activity threatens island states with flood and fertile areas with prolonged drought. Some critics have proclaimed the death of nature. People judge that environmental degradation is not only irritating, inconvenient, disappointing, or unfortunate, but immoral, bad, wrong or evil. Human civilization is threatened. Environmental problems have adverse impacts on human health and well-being. Natural resources are destroyed which have important economic, scientific, medical, recreational and aesthetic uses. The development of knowledge, the refinement of culture, and the creation of new forms of aesthetic expression depend on the preservation of nature. Nature is a source of inspiration, an object of contemplation, a material precondition for civilized life. Nature is an organic, dynamic whole. Nature has intrinsic value. Exhibiting hubris, philistinism, vandalism is ethically deficient.

REFERENCES

1. Worster, Donald. *The Wealth of Nature: Environmental History and the Ecological Imagination*. New York: Oxford University Press, 1993.
2. Sri Aurobindo, *The Future Evolution of Man: The Divine Life upon Earth*. 2nd sub-edition. Wisconsin: Lotus Press, 2003.
3. Cless, Downing. "Ecologically Conjuring Doctor Faustus." *Journal of Dramatic Theory and Criticism*. Spring 2006. Volume XX, Number 2.

4. Des Jardins, J. *Environmental Ethics*. Belmont: Wadsworth Publishing Company, 1997.
5. Fromm, Harold. *The Nature of Being Human: From Environmentalism to Consciousness*. Baltimore: The Johns Hopkins University Press, 2009.
6. The Real World Coalition. *The Politics of the Real World*. London: Earthscan, 1998.
7. Glotfelty, Cheryll, and Harold Fromm. *The Ecocriticism Reader: Landmarks in Literary Ecology*. Athens, Georgia: The University of Georgia Press, 1996.
8. Dooling, D.M., and Smith, P.J., eds. *I Become Part of It*. New York: Harper Collins, 1989.
9. Bright, April. "Burn Grass" in *Country in Flames*. Canberra: Department of the Environment, Sport and Territories, 1995.
10. Jackson, Moana. *The Maori and the Criminal Justice System*, Part 2, Wellington: Department of Justice, 1988.
11. Dwivedi, O.P. "Classical India" in *A Companion to Environmental Philosophy*. ed. Jamieson, Dale. Oxford: Blackwell Publishing, 2003.
12. Datta, M.N., trans. *Mahabharata*. Delhi: Parimal Publications, 1988.
13. Thoreau, H.D., *Walden*. London: Dent, 1992.
14. Burnet, J. *Platonis Opera*. Oxford: Oxford University Press, 1900.
15. Bekker, E. *Aristotelis Opera*. Berlin: Walter de Gruyter, 1960.
16. Orr, David. *Earth in Mind: On Education, Environment, and the Human Prospect*. 2nd revised edition. Washington: Island Press, 2004.
17. Lincoln, Abraham. *Great Speeches*. Pittsburgh: General Press, 2012.
18. Gore, Albert. *Earth in the Balance: Forging a New Common Purpose*. London: Earthscan, 2007.

2

Cheryll Glotfelty

Cheryll Glotfelty (Born-1958)
The co-editor of The Ecocriticism Reader

Cheryll Burgess Glotfelty is Associate Professor of Literature and Environment in the University of Nevada at Reno, United States of America. She has written several essays on ecocriticism, Women Writers and Western American Literature. She co-edited with Harold Fromm *The Ecocriticism Reader: Landmarks in Literary Ecology* University of Georgia Press, 1996, that helped green the field of literary studies. Her most intense interest is the connection between literature and the environment. She promulgated the concept of "ecocriticism." She produced an anthology of ecocritical essays. She has become the first American professor of literature and the environment.

Cheryll Glotfelty is an avid reader, nature lover and concerned planetary citizen. University of Nevada, Reno, hired her as the nation's first Professor of Literature and Environment in 1990. Cheryll Glotfelty is the co-founder and past president of the Association for the Study of Literature and Environment

(ASLE). Her commitment to teaching has been recognized with many teaching awards including the CASE Carnegie Professor of the Year Award for Nevada. She published essays on Rachel Carson, Terry Tempest Williams, Susan Griffin, Willa Cather, Peter Berg, Ecocriticism, Nuclear Landscapes, Bioregionalism, Western American Literature, and Pedagogy.

Her most recent book co-edited with Tom Lynch and Karla Armbruster, is *The Bioregional Imagination: Literature, Ecology and Place* in 2012. It inspires to think about place and planet from an ecological perspective. She wrote *Literary Nevada: Writings from the Silver State* in 2008. It is the first comprehensive anthology of Nevada Literature. Her aim is to display the state's rich literary heritage and to cultivate a love of place among residents.

Cheryll Glotfelty is currently working on an ecocritical biography of documentary landscape photographer Peter Goin. Peter Goin has photographed nuclear landscapes, post-mining sites, and water in the arid West. Cheryll, her husband, Steve, and daughter, Rosa, live at "Scorpion Acres" with three horses, a donkey, two cats, two parakeets, goldfish, and a dozen free-range peacocks.

Ecocriticism is the literary response to the most pressing contemporary issue of all, the global environmental crisis. Ecological approach to literary studies is an environmental perspective in contemporary literary studies. We have been living in an age of environmental crisis. Literature responds to the contemporary issues and events. Until very recently literary studies has become aware of the environmental cred humanities disciplines, like history, philosophy, law, sociology and religion have been greening since 1970s.

Social movements, like the civil rights movement and women's liberation movement of the sixties and seventies, have transformed literary studies. Ecological criticism has been developing since the 1970s.

Birth of Ecocriticism

The field of environmental literary criticism was planted in 1980s. Frederick O. Waage edited *Teaching Environmental*

Literature: Materials, Methods, Resources which fosters environmental concern and awareness in literary studies. Alicia Nitecki founded *The American Nature Writing Newsletter* in 1989, who published brief essays, book reviews, classroom notes, and information related to the writing on nature and the environment. University of Nevada, Reno, created the first academic position in Literature and the Environment. Several special sessions on nature writing or environmental literature appeared on the programmes of annual literary conferences. Harold Fromm organized the 1991 special session entitled "Ecocriticism: The Greening of Literary Studies." The 1992 American Literature Association symposium was chaired by Glen Love entitled "American Nature Writing: New Contexts, New Approaches." In 1992, at the annual meeting of the Western Literature Association, a new Association for the Study of Literature and Environment (ASLE) was formed, with Scott Slovic elected first president. ASLE's mission is: "to promote the exchange of ideas and information pertaining to literature that considers the relationship between human beings and the natural world."

Ecological literary study emerged as a recognizable critical school by 1993. The fundamental premise of the ecological criticism is that human culture is intimately connected to the physical world. Human culture affects the physical world and is affected by it. Ecocritics examine human perception of wilderness. They also explore the transformation of human perception of nature in the course of the history. They find out whether current environmental issues are accurately represented or even mentioned in popular culture and modern literature.

Civil Rights and Women's Liberation Movements have transformed literary studies. Environmental concerns have profoundly influenced humanities disciplines, like, literature, history, philosophy, law and sociology since the 1970s. Individual literary and cultural scholars have been developing ecological criticism since the seventies. They did not organize a group like other subjects. Hence their efforts were not recognized as belonging to a distinct critical school or movement.

William Rueckert may have been the first person to use the term "ecocriticism" (Barry, 240). In 1978, Rueckert published an essay titled *Literature and Ecology: An Experiment in Ecocriticism*. He argues the use of ecology and ecological concepts to the study of literature. Ecocriticism is an organized movement to study literature from the environmental perspective. British Marxist critic, Raymond Williams wrote a seminal critique of pastoral literature in 1973, *The Country and the City*. He observed that losses lamented in pastoral might be true ones. He professed a green socialism.

Ecocriticism is distinct from other critical approaches. Literary theory generally examines the relations between writers, texts, and the world. The current environmental problems are largely of our own making—a by-product of culture. Ecocriticism explores the link between the human life and the environment.

Historian Donald Worster observed the connection between the contemporary global environmental crisis and the function of ethical systems. If people overlook ecological values, the quality of human life in the country suffers. Ecologic crisis is the product of the democratic culture. Settlement influenced Native American ways of thinking about nature. Industrial revolution again remade the ecology, economy and conceptions of nature in the region. European explorers and settlers arrived in America during the seventeenth century. Carolyn Merchant analysed these two transformations in *Ecological Revolutions: Nature, Gender and Science in New England*. Merchant argues that past ways of relating to the land could become an inspiration for renewing resources and achieving sustainability in the future. Past ways of relating to land will help people to establish ethical relationship with nature in the context of globalization, climate change and privatization.

Ecocriticism opposes the exploitative development. The ecological analysis of the human life reflected in literature has been called ecological Criticism or Ecocriticism. The critical theory deals with the relationship between the human life and the nature. It transcends the exclusive categories of centre and periphery. It is the high time now to ponder over the evil consequences of industrialization and mechanization, globalization, privatization and liberalization. It is the study of the interrelationship between nature and human life.

Ecological approach to literature emerged in our postmodern age. It takes into account the contemporary global environmental crisis. Race, class and gender were the crucial topics of the late twentieth century.

Earth's life support system has come under stress. Literary study has become preoccupied with the environmental concerns in the twenty-first century.

Definition of Ecocriticism

Ecocriticism is the study of the relationship between literature and the physical environment. Just as feminist criticism examines language and literature from a feminist perspective, and Marxist criticism brings an awareness of modes of production and economic class to its analysis of texts, ecocriticism is a nature centered approach to literary studies. Ecocritics and theorists study the representation of nature in the sonnet. They examine the role of physical setting in the plot of the novel, drama and short story. They examine consistency of the values expressed in the play with ecological wisdom. In addition to race, class, and gender, Ecocritics have added a new critical category called 'place'. They explore the ways literature affected human kind's relationship to the natural world. Science itself is open to literary analysis.

Ecocriticism is broad in its scope. The fundamental premise of the Ecocriticism is that human culture is connected to the physical world, affecting it and affected by it. An interconnection between nature and culture is the subject of Ecocriticism. Ecocriticism is distinct from other critical approaches. We should agree with Barry Commoner's first law of ecology, "Everything is connected to everything else." Joseph Meeker introduced the term literary ecology in *The Comedy of Survival: Studies in Literary Ecology* published in 1972. He referred the term of literary ecology to "the study of biological themes and relationships which appear in literary works. It is simultaneously an attempt to discover what roles have been played by literature in the ecology of the human species."[1] We should not acknowledge that Literature is disconnected from the reality in the world. It plays an important role in the immensely complex world. It demystifies the reality in the world.

William Rueckert used the term Ecocriticism for the examination of literary works by using ecology and ecological concepts. Human actions have been damaging the planet's life support systems. We are responsible in a large extent for contemporary environmental problems. We should change our way of life, otherwise we will lose most of the natural beauty and biodiversity which has enriched our life. Currently other terms like ecopoetics, environmental literary criticism, and green cultural studies are used to refer to the study of interconnection between nature and human life.

Donald Worster, the historian has explained that culture plays a role in the maintenance or destruction of environment:

> We are facing a global crisis today, not because of how ecosystems function but rather because of how our ethical systems function. Getting through the crisis requires understanding our impact on nature as precisely as possible, but even more, it requires understanding those ethical systems and using that understanding to reform them. Historians, along with literary scholars, anthropologists, and philosophers, cannot do the reforming, of course, but they can help with the understanding. (*The Wealth of Nature,* p. 27)[2]

Worster and other historians have been writing environmental histories. They explain the reciprocal relationship between humans and land. They do not look towards nature just as a stage for human actions but as an actor. They have observed that environmental conditions, economic modes of production, and cultural values are interconnected. Anthropologists have noticed the connection between culture and geography. Value systems and environmental conditions help cultures survive. Contemporary psychologists have explored the link between environmental conditions and mental health. They regard that modern estrangement from nature is the basis of our social and psychological ills. They have also regarded that the main reason for contemporary social and psychological ills is the society's estrangement from nature. Environmental ethics, deep ecology, Ecofeminism, social ecology have emerged in Philosophy to study the causes of environmental degradation. These new subfields in philosophy formulate an alternative view of life which will establish healthy relationship with the earth. Most of the religions in the world contain much wisdom about nature and spirituality. Interdisciplinary approach helps to understand the causes of environmental crisis. Our fragmented, compartmentalized and overspecialized way of knowing the world is also contributed for the destruction of the nature.

Ecocriticism studies how nature is represented in literature. It raises the consciousness. It has promulgated Nature writing which teaches us to value the natural world. Nature writing has a rich past, a vibrant present, and a promising future. Ecocritics study the environmental conditions of an author's life—the influence of place on the imagination of the author. They demonstrate that the place where an author grew up traveled and wrote is helpful in understanding his or her work. Ecocritics have proposed the theory that human cannot be separated from nature. Ecofeminism, a theoretical discourse explores the link between exploitation of women and the domination of nature.

The Future of Ecocriticism

Ecocriticism has the power to change the world. It raises our consciousness regarding nature. It explores the relationship between humans and nature. It has become a multi-ethnic movement. There is a strong connection between the environment and issues of social justice. Environmental problems are global. Worldwide collaboration on the reforestation will solve the problem. Ecocriticism has become visible and influential recently. It is an important approach to literary study. It helps the readers to see the world in a new way. It opens the doors of understanding nature. Like feminism, Ecocriticism has developed through three major phases. Ecocritics study the relationship between human culture and the physical world. They examine the representations of nature in fiction and drama. They also analyse the environmental literature in eastern and western countries. Harold Fromm has speculated that industrial revolution has influenced humanity's relationship to nature. He warned that technology has created the fast illusion that we control nature; we should remember that our "unconquerable minds" are vitally dependent upon natural support systems. Linguistic and aesthetic competence forms our interactions with nature. Neil Evernden argues that ecocriticism has revolutionized our sense of self. He said that "there is no such thing as an individual, only an individual in context. There is no such thing as self, only self-in-place."[3] Joseph W. Meeker, an ethnologist and a scholar of comparative literature regards literary production as an important characteristic of the human species. He has compared literary production among humans with flight in birds or radar bats. He asserts that literature influences human behaviour and our attitude to nature. Literature plays an important role in the welfare and survival of mankind. It gives a valuable insight into human relationships, with other species and with the world around us.

Joseph D. Meeker considers that from an ecological point of view the literary mode comedy promotes healthy survival values while tragedy is maladaptive. He praises those authors who exemplify a strong sense of nature through their writing. Sanders observed that contemporary critically acclaimed fiction lacks an awareness of the natural world. He said it is the result of the blindness of our culture at large. Glen A. Love emphasized the need of redirecting ourselves from ego-consciousness to "eco-consciousness." Only nature-oriented literature can do this. Thoreau, John Muir and Ado Leopold all of them tried to instill a land ethic. Russian philosopher and literary critic Mikhail Bakhtin's literary theories provide an ideal perspective for ecocritics.

Part one of *The Ecocriticism Reader: Landmarks in Literary Ecology* is entitled as "Ecotheory: Reflections on Nature and Culture".

Aldous Huxley explained man's unnatural treatment of nature and its sad results. All forms of life modify their contexts. Changes in human ways often affect nonhuman. The advent of automobile eliminated huge flocks of sparrows. Lynn White, Jr. in his famous essay "The Historical Roots of Our Ecologic Crisis" argues that the environmental crisis is basically a matter of the beliefs and values that direct science and technology. If we overlook ecological values, our quality of life is affected. He censures Judeo-Christian religion for its anthropocentric arrogance and dominating position towards nature. Aldous Huxley argued that Man's unnatural treatment of nature has brought sad results for the humanity at large. All forms of life modify their contexts. Man is not an exception. He has affected his environment notably. Human actions often affect non-human nature. If people overlook ecologic values, the quality of human life is deteriorated.

Changes in human ways often affect non-human nature. People have often been the dynamic element in their own environment. We cannot neglect the responsibility for natural environment. Hydrogen bomb poses a severe threat to all life forms on earth. A war fought with the hydrogen bomb might alter the genetics of all life on the earth. Unplanned urbanization, ill execution of the government policies has posed a problem in establishing a just social order. Lynn White has given the account of the nature of science and technology and their impact on the present ecology. Democratic culture also contributed to the ecologic crisis. Thoughts of the people determine their relationship with the landscape. Religion also plays the crucial role it teaches the people beliefs regarding nature and destiny.

Formerly man had been part of nature. Now he has become the exploiter of nature. Science and technology both are blessed words in our contemporary time. Science and technology have grown out of attitudes towards man's relation to nature. More science and more technology are not going to help us solve the present problem of ecologic crisis. We should find the solution in rethinking and refeeling nature. Saint Francis of Assisi, the greatest radical in Christian history since Christ, believed in the virtue of humility—not merely for the individual but for man as a species.

The present increasing disruption of the global environment is the product of a dynamic technology and science, originated in the western medieval world. We must reject the axiom that nature exists to serve human beings. Lynn White proposes Saint Francis as a patron saint for ecologists.

Lynn White observes that Christianity is the most anthropocentric religion the world has ever seen. Christianity teaches the people that God has created the earth and all its plants, animals, birds and fish for man's benefit and rule. No item in the physical creation had other purpose than serving Man. God had made the Nature. Nature can reveal the divine mentality. Lynn White Jr. very categorically said that ecologic crisis cannot be solved merely by applying more science and technology. Dynamic technology and science have contributed largely for the present disruption of the global environment.

The greatest spiritual revolutionary in Western history, Saint Francis, proposed an alternative view of nature and man's relation to it. He tried to substitute the idea of the equality of all creatures, for the idea of man's infinite rule of creation. Roots of our ecologic trouble are largely religious; the remedy must also be essentially religious. Lynn White, Jr. proposed Francis as a patron saint for ecologists. We must rethink and refeel our nature and destiny.

Christopher Manes considers silence of nature in "Nature and Silence." Nature is silent in Western culture. The status of being a speaking subject is considered a human privilege. At the very outset Manes points out that nature is silent in anthropocentric cultures. George Lukacs said that "nature is a societal category."[4]

Animistic cultures see the natural world as inspirited. Not are people inspirited but animals, plants, rivers and stones too. Humans interact and communicate with non-human objects. Entities such as animals, plants, rivers, stones in nature are perceived as articulate. They are able to communicate with humans. People in animistic cultures regard nature as alive and articulate. The attitude of nature which regards nature as alive and articulate has consequences in the realm of social practices. Knowledge about nature is significant for the progress of institutions. Michel Foucault has demonstrated that "social power operates through a regime of privileged speakers, having historical embodiments as priests and kings, authors, intellectuals, and celebrities."[5] The words of these speakers are taken seriously. The discourse of the silenced speakers such as women, children, prisoner and insane are regarded as meaningless. Hans Peter Duerr argued that "people do not exploit a nature that speaks to them."[6] A viable environmental ethic can help to protect nature and can establish communication with nature. We must stop the environmentally destructive practices. We must establish communication between human subjects and the natural world. To regard nature as alive and articulate is the indication of a viable culture.

Modern society must rethink and refeel nature and reestablish the communication with nature. Industrial revolution has profoundly changed Man's relation with Nature. Formerly man had been part of nature, he became exploiter of nature. Kant rightly said that our exclusive preoccupation with reason has furthered excesses of political power and self-interest. Foucault has put it, "We should not need to wait for bureaucracy or concentration camps to recognize the existence of such relations."[7] Institutions involved in environmental destruction need to be changed. The easy alliance of power and reason has supported the institutions involved in natural destruction and their discourses. Most of the contemporary discourses based on reason have made nature silent and instrumental.

Heidegger has rightly said that all languages both reveals and conceals.[8] Our language has concealed nature largely. We must begin to use the language of ecological humility. Animism is universal in human history. Animism believes that the entire world is inspired and alive including cultural artifacts and non-human world. Animistic societies have been looking after nature always. Institutions in Middle Ages have regarded nature as the symbol for the glory and orderliness of God. There are discourses which respect or abuse nature. Deep ecology reevaluates the silence of nature which has been imposed by human discourse based on reason. Evolutionary theory has often been used to justify humanity's domination of nature. Man is regarded as the zenith of evolution because of his brain size, self-consciousness or some other privileged quality. Christopher Manes has emphatically said "There is no higher or lower, first or second, better or worse life forms. There is only the unfolding of life form after life form, more or less genealogically related, each with a mix of characteristics."

Biocentrism rejects the exclusive concern for the *Homo sapiens*. Humanism has placed Man at the highest place in the animal hierarchy. Deep Ecology has painted an alternate picture of the world. Humanistic scale of values regards fungus as the lowliest of forms. Ecologists have brought to the notice that health of forests depends on *Mycorrhizal* fungus. If fungus were to go extinct tomorrow, it will be catastrophic for the entire biosphere. The disappearance of the forests would bring massive changes in hydrology, atmosphere, and temperature. Human freedom, worth and purpose can be protected only by strengthening and appreciating non-human life forms on the earth. Ethics implies the way we talk about the world, the way we perceive it. Deep ecologists have taught us a new language of ontological egalitarianism. We should be free from the obsession of regarding Man as the preeminent creature in the world. We should promote an understanding of, and reverence for, and dialogue with nature rather than soliloquies. Today we need to cultivate a refined sense of human limitation and respect for otherness.

Christopher Manes has expressed the view that the time has come for Man to accept His humble position in the order of the natural world. Man is one species among millions of other beautiful, terrible, fascinating—and signifying life forms. A viable environmental ethic is the characteristic of a standard culture. Nature should be a speaking subject in our culture.

Harold Fromm in "From Transcendence to Obsolescence: A Route Map" describes the effects of industrial revolution on Culture Nature relationship. He warned that technology has created a false illusion among the public that people can control nature. The fact is that Man is dependent upon natural support systems.

The rise of industrialisation by the eighteenth century in the west is responsible for the decline of religion in some extent. Industrialisation has brought many comforts to the ordinary man, like comfortable houses, medicines, rapid communication through time and space, etc. Industrial revolution has altered humanity's perception of nature. Irrespective of being amidst of luxuries and comforts, modern man feels alienated, empty, without purpose and direction. Harold Fromm expressed the need to establish healthy relationship with nature now. Nature nurtures Man and all other life forms. Fromm has explained the myth of omnipotence and illogical attack of industrial corporations who attack the basic conception of environmental protection. Man has become oblivious of his roots in the earth or unwilling to acknowledge them. Polluted air causes traumatic effect on human lives. Environmental crisis is not ecological but ontological too. One of the readers has asked Harold Fromm the question: "Do we destroy our economy: eliminate many necessities of life; go back to living in tents for the sake of clean air?"[9] As a reply to the reader Fromm explained that for the biological existence of Man, nature acts as the grounds of life. He expressed the need that Man should stop shocking, and suicidal disregard of his roots in the earth.

Alan Drengston, editor of the deep ecology journal, *The Trumpeter,* has established the Ecostery Project, which hopes to revitalize a medieval social form: monasteries whose function is to support an understanding of, and reverence for, and dialogue with nature. Medieval discourse for all its absurdities revealed a refined sense of human limitation and respect for other creatures; we must cherish these values today. Natural word has been voiceless and subjectless in fiction. We must restore ourselves to the humbler status of *Homo sapiens*: one species among millions of other beautiful, terrible, fascinating and signifying forms. We can introduce nature in our culture to solve the present problem of ecologic ruin.

Frederick Turner in "Cultivating the American Garden" has discussed the issue of the definition of nature and natural. According to Turner nature is dangerous, pure and innocent yet wise. It is the only real touchstone of what is good and what is beautiful. We must behave in a responsible manner towards nature. We should avoid being merely derivative. We should adopt ecological modesty which asserts that we are only one species among many. We do not enjoy any special rights. We should serve for the greater glory and beauty of the world.

Alison Byerly wrote the brilliant essay, "The Uses of Landscape." She has drawn attention towards aesthetic and picturesque view of nature. The aestheticisation of landscape has made it an object of consumption. A harmonious relationship between man and nature is a prerequisite for a viable culture.

In America natural areas have diminished. The people perceive that National Park can provide them wilderness experience. Wilderness areas offer outstanding opportunities for solitude. La Pague and Ranney have rightly argued in an article that we must, "understand our cultural as well as economical ties to the land."[10] Most of the creative artists are influenced by nature. Environmental philosophers have attributed nature an inherent value of its own, independent of its uses. Alison Byrely insists that natural world should satisfy aesthetic sensibilities of the people. We do not create the wilderness but it makes and remakes itself. We should learn nature's text as something other than fiction. Political and economic structures must acknowledge and maintain the world's most valuable ecosystems. Ecocriticism describes the relationship between nature and culture. Ecocriticism draws heavily from four other disciplines: ecology, ethics, language, and criticism. Language theory examines how words represent human and non-human life. Criticism judges the quality and integrity of works and promotes their dissemination. Darwin said that time is deep and change is deep.

In the twentieth century, people recognized that their pattern of growth can destroy natural resources. Those losses gave people a new sense of land and the intricate relations it supports. Ecology offers to culture an ethic for survival in the darker moments of history. Industrial growth coincided with the environmental loss. Ecocriticism examines natural and cultural interactions. Ecology can heal a sick world. Rachel Carson through social discourse in her landmark work, *Silent Spring* (1962) aroused a sense of conscience about pesticides that poison ground water and annihilate biodiversity. Ecopatriots in the 1970s attacked anthropocentric forces-military, political, technological; profit-making people that defamed the true course of evolution. Deep ecologists have called for the revival of public ethics and green policies. They also considered that ethical choices affect land and people. Eco-historians explained that the contact between Native Americans and explorers as a clash and land and sea-based values. Human beings can learn many things from the land. Literary texts reflect how a civilization regards its natural heritage. Scientific and literary modes of analysis are parallel. In science we know the truth through data and in literature we know through metaphor. There are no natural limits to the literary criticism. Literature borrows from science images for utopist and dystopic writing.

Science fiction writers forecast ecological collapse. They imitate the theory and experiments of science yet challenge its inherent faith in progress. Ecocritics regard that science presents solutions that generate only new problems. Marxist critics believe that economics determine social history. Therefore according to them, capitalism is the source of all conflict, oppression and environmental abuse. The fact cannot be neglected that disturbance is common. Aborigines and socialists have often contributed for the environmental loss. Physical conditions affect beliefs. Ecocriticism expresses the hope that flawed social condition may be improved by strengthening environmental condition and economic condition. New historicists have not understood the significance of nature in shaping culture. Their biased view is that culture is entirely conditioned by race, gender, class, money, and other factors of material social life. Lewis Thomas rightly proposed that the core of life is language. Ecocriticism provides the view that social constructions like gender, race and class are conditioned by use and abuse of land. As land is traded, people are degraded. Ecocritics focus on the idea that place defines social status.

Edward O. Wilson, in *The Diversity of Life* has given an overview of biodiversity and accounted for the urgent environmental stewardship.

Raymond Williams' *The Country and the City* guided a generation of scholars in environmental history. Thoreau has given the account that Nature moulds the people spiritually and physically. Joshua Meyrowitz in *No Sense of Place: The Impact of Electronic Media on Social Behaviour* argued that television and computers have created cultures no longer shaped by physical location. Joseph W. Meeker in *The Comedy of Survival: Studies in Literary Ecology* examines human-environment relation and asks for living with the natural order.

Neil Evernden wrote the influential essay, "Beyond Ecology" she explicates that we should not justify the existence of non-human nature on the basis of utility but its inherent value. We should preserve and conserve nature; it only safeguards us from consequences of development processes. She proposed that things are interrelated—change in one affects the other. There are no discrete entities. She argued that "How can the proper study for man be man if it is impossible for man to exist out of context?" We should not deal with just the fragment. Edith Cobb has explicated that child's relationship with the land is aesthetic.[11] According to John Dewey the aesthetic experience lies in the relationship between the individual and the environment. Role of the environment in the life of the individual is profoundly important. Individual is a component of the environment, not something distinct from it. Organisms are intimately related with the environment in which they live. World is not just the set of resources. Northrop Frye proposed that the goal of the arts is "recapture, in full consciousness, that original lost sense of identity with our surroundings, where there is nothing outside the mind of the man, or something identical with the mind of man." Nature is animate because we are a part of it. Northrop Frye rightly said that genuine joy human beings can get when they establish an association between the mind and the outside world. The act of naming is a part of the process of establishing a sense of place.

Nell Evernden believes that there is some connection between the individual and his particular place. Paul Shepard says knowing "who you are impossible without knowing where you are from."[12] The significance of a place is a very personal thing. Man cannot and should not be studied exclusive of his environment. The beauty and complexity of nature is continuous with man. Man and nature are not only interrelated but interdependent. Arts involves in the study of the interrelatedness and the close and fundamental involvement of self with place. Preservation of non-human is a very personal struggle. There no such thing as an individual. Individual can be known in context. Individual is a constituent of place. Individual is defined and conditioned by place.

"Literature and Ecology" is a very significant critical essay written by William Rueckert. Ecocriticism is the application of ecology and ecological concepts to the study of literature. Ecocriticism is relevant to the present and future of the world we all live in. Ecocritics like Rueckert are trying to develop an ecological poetics by applying ecological concepts to the reading, teaching, and writing about literature. Ecological study of literature opens ways for the human community from destroying the natural community, and with it the human community because environmental destruction involves the destruction of human community entirely. Ecologists illuminate that the present attitude of the people towards nature is self-destructive. Ecocritics explore the grounds upon which the human, the non-human can coexist, cooperate, and flourish in the biosphere. Most of the ecologists such as Aldo Leopold, Ian McHarg, and Barry Commoner have developed ecological vision which can be translated into social, economic, political, and individual programmes. All these ecological visions are far-reaching and rebellious. They subvert the continued growth economy which dominates all emerging and most developed industrial states. A balanced or sustainable state economy, with an entirely new concept of development, is central to all ecological visions. Commoner's first law of ecology is common to all ecologists and ecological visions. Commoner put forth the view that, "Everything is connected to everything else." Ecological vision is not mind blowing but mind expanding. Man is not free to do anything what he wants to do with nature. Ecological vision involves the idea that nature should be protected by human laws.

William Rueckert regards poems as part of energy pathways which sustain life. Literary world and the natural world sustain life and communities. The poem is a stored energy. Reading and teaching of poetry releases the flow of energy that may flow through the human community. In literature, all energy comes from the creative imagination. Energy stored in a poem can be used as renewable source of energy. William Rueckert appeals to form some connections between teaching literature and the health of the biosphere.

Kenneth Burke has rightly said that literary works raise the energy levels of students in the classrooms. In the ecosphere, one life process is interdependent upon another. Earth's life support systems are mutually interconnected. A strong nature can keep culture healthy and viable. Anthropocentric vision has become tragic flaw of the contemporary people. The world needs an ecological poetics. People should adopt ecological vision. Rueckert while explicating the importance of ecological vision referred to a fine old adage, "Where there is no ecological vision, the people will perish." William Rueckert said emphatically that poems can be studied as models for energy flow, community building, and ecosystems. Literary works like plays, poems, novels raise the energy levels of the readers. The motives of creativity and community can be achieved through literary texts. Barry Commoner has rightly pointed out, "this literary heritage has not been enough to save us from ecological disaster." He also made an important suggestion that there is the need of unity of vision and action, knowledge and power. Rueckert has emphasized the harshest and cruelest reality of our time, "Real power in our time is political, economic, and technological; real knowledge is increasingly scientific." Literature should be at the centre of all. He has analysed the situation clearly:

> ...We are in an environmental crisis because the means by which we use the ecosphere to produce wealth are destructive of the ecosystem itself. The present system of production is self-destructive. The present course of human civilization is suicidal. In our unwitting march toward ecological suicide we have run out of options. Human beings have broken out of the circle of life, driven not by biological need, but by social organization which they have devised to conquer nature....

Margaret Atwood's novel *Surfacing* is full of ecological wisdom. She has drawn an analogy between the ways in which men treat and destroy women and the ways in which men treat and destroy nature. W.S. Merwin has written a classic ecological text, *Lice*. He told that if human beings do not change their way of life which is self-destructive, it will be disastrous for the entire biosphere. Merwin and Adrienne Rich have called for inner transformation of human beings as the most urgent necessity, for avoiding destruction of the world and the survival of the human life.

Sueellen Campbell wrote "The Land and Language of Desire." He proposed that ecocritical values are life enhancing. Nature writers often say that aboriginal cultures are better than the western cultures. They have always lived in perfect harmony with nature. Ecocriticism questions the concepts on which the old hierarchies are built. Barry Lopez has rightly pointed that human imagination as well as human action has always interacted with the land. The concept of biocentrism in ecology is very important. Biocentrism means that human beings are neither superior nor worse than other creatures. They are equivalent to the whole lot of creatures in nature.

Terry Eagleton has argued in *Literary Theory* that all criticism is political. He said that critic should first of all decide what change they want to bring in the present system of the world, later they may choose the appropriate strategies to realize the objective. Literary theory assumes that all readings are situated. We always read within a system. Social, political, economic, cultural and personal circumstances influence our reading and understanding the texts. Lopez has told in *Arctic Dreams* that our thinking of landscape is conditioned by our knowledge, our imagination, and our character. Lopez has written about intimacy between the land and the people. Preservation and stability are the central words in ecology. Everything is connected, nothing is isolated. Human beings are part of vast networks. Sueellen Campbell rightly argued that nature and culture are not opposites, but they are interdependent and interconnected. He said:

> ...Because our culture does not teach us that we are plain citizens of the earth, because we live apart from the natural world and deny our sympathy with it, we have lost the sense of unity that is still possible in other cultures. Our desire marks what we have lost and what we still hope to regain. Desire, for ecology, goes beyond humanity. He also argued that human beings belong not only to the networks of language and culture but also to the networks of land.

David Mazel addressed the problem of heterogeneity of literature and the close relationship between ecocriticism, environmental literature, and environmental politics in his famous critical essay, "American Literary Environmentalism as Domestic Orientalism." Mazel proposes that heterogeneity of literature and the interconnections between ecocriticism, environmental literature and environmental politics are not the problems. They are necessary for the survival of the society, and they are the constituents of the environment. Environmentalism is one of the potential modes for exercising power. According to Mazel environment is not just a stage to be acted upon but itself a performer and an actor. Construction of environment itself is the exercise of cultural power. According to Mazel, American literary environmentalism is a domestic orientalism.

According to Mazel emergent political environmentalism are not entirely a new system of beliefs, thoughts, and ideas. It is a refinement of earlier structures of knowledge, political, economic, and cultural system. Science fiction like all other fiction writing describes what is happening in the world. It gives an insight into people's actions and feelings. It also describes the relationship between people and their environment. Joseph W. Meeker has written a very influential essay, "The Comic Mode." He proposes that literature is essentially an imitation of human action. Doctrine of *mimesis* was first stated in Plato's *Republic* and later it was revised in Aristotle's *Poetics.* He has explicated the difference between comic and tragic view of life through the examples of Sophocles and John Barth. Both of them have imitated the same action that is the revelation of Oedipus's crimes. Sophocles exemplifies the tragic view of life whereas Barth shows comic view of the same action. Tragic artist imitates man as a noble creature. Barth has shown man's innate stupidity and ignorance. He emphasises the triviality of human passions. The protagonist in tragedy organizes the power of mind and spirit to rise above the predicament he is placed in. But he cannot come out of the problem because of flaw in his character. Tragic hero is always in conflict with forces superior to him. These forces are nature, the gods, moral law, passionate love, the greatness of ideas and knowledge. These forces determine the welfare or suffering of the tragic hero.

Comedy is universal. The comedy demonstrates irrational behaviour of human beings. The comic heroes commit follies which reveal their essential ignorance and ridiculousness. Aristotle put it that comedy imitates the actions of men who are subnormal or inferior to the social norm and tragedy imitates the superior men. Political philosophy has failed to address simple questions in human life. The comic hero survives the situation. The tragic hero dies for his ideals. The tragic view of man has led to cultural and natural disasters. Comedy concerns with man's capacity for survival and the continuity of life. Literary comedy depicts the loss of equilibrium and its recovery. The comedy reveals the importance of life. It encourages life even though it is meaningless.

Joseph W. Meeker expresses the view that human beings must accommodate to the forces that surround human life. We must learn the lesson of accommodating others from other more stable comic heroes of life. According to Oscar Wilde, the nineteenth century British playwright, present models of human behaviour. Tragic hero shows people how to bear loss magnificently.

Joseph W. Meeker expressed the appropriate view that man is a part of nature. He is subject to all natural limitations and flaws. He says that proper study of mankind is survival. Comic strategy sees life as game. Ecological view of life is modest, heroic and simple. Meeker suggested that human should cultivate a new mentality capable of understanding intricate processes of nature. Comedy illustrates that man survival of the human species depends upon his ability to change himself and capacity to accept the limitations. Comedy teaches people the values of humility and endurance. Ecological wisdom should be cherished by mankind for the betterment of human and non-human life. Ecological wisdom can help the existence of many species including the human, and the continuity of biological environment.

Annette Kolodny wrote "Unearthing Herstory." He emphasized that the relationship between nature and culture are subtle. Ecocriticism promises a better future. John Mitchell in, "Big Yellow Taxi" said: You don't know what you've got till it gone; they paved paradise and put up a parking lot. Ecocriticism is a revolt against culture based on toil, domination, and self-denial. American poet, Charles Hansford stated ecological vision through poetry:

To strive with nature little it avails.
Her favors to improve and nicely scan
Is all that is within the reach of Man.
Nature is to be follow'd, and not for forc'd,
For, otherwise, our labor will be lost.[13]

Kolodny suggested that the will to freedom, the will to community, the desire for self-fulfillment, the passive acceptance, are the pastoral which play very crucial role in the formation of the sustainable society.

Scott Russell Sanders proposes in "Speaking a Word for Nat" environment plays a crucial role in shaping human life. He calls much contemporary American fiction barren because it does not acknowledge the influence of nature on human actions and perceptions. Setting of the action plays a significant role in the development of events and characters in the novels of Thomas Hardy. Scott Russell pointed out that recent fiction lacks any sense of nature, any acknowledgement of a non-human context. Mainstream of British fiction also lacks acknowledgement of non-human context. In the British mainstream fiction nature does not play a powerful role.

Sanders explain that in the great works of American literature the human world is set against the overarching background of nature. Landscape in American literature is not just scenery, not a flimsy stage. It energizes human lives. Human lives are bounded to nature and measured by it.

American writers like Melville, Hawthorne, Cooper and Thoreau have explored human life in the context of nature. Sanders observed that nature awareness is conspicuously absent in the contemporary fiction. Lawrence believes that land is holy; it is the source of meaning and energy. Emerson's *Nature* (1836) is the most eloquent manifesto of the attitude to contemporary world. Thoreau portrayed a dynamic nature in *Walden.* The central view common to all nature writers is that human life is continuous with the life of nature. Wendell Berry in *A Place on Earth* argues that nature is the medium through which life transpires. He emphasized that nature is the prime source of value, meaning and purpose of human life. Mainstream fiction has not shown a deep awareness of nature. Neglect of nature is a shared blindness in culture at large. Sanders said that contemporary people in the midst of luxuries have lost the direct contact with the organic world. Contemporary people treat environment in the shabby manner. Durable art enlarges the vision of the people. Art that matters has never reproduced the superficial consciousness of the age. Writers like DeLillo, Carvet, Mason and their less able imitators are reporting our own condition surrounded by artificiality and illiteracy of nature. Cervantes, Melville, Faulkner, Garcia Marquez and the host of other writers have enlarged our vision of life by incorporating human life with nature through their writing.

People's imagination of land and its creatures play a decisive role in the way of their life. Sanders rightly commented on ecological vision and human life:

However accurately it reflects the surface of our times, fiction that never looks beyond the human realm is profoundly false, and therefore pathological. No matter how urban our experience, no matter how oblivious we may be toward nature, we are nonetheless animals, two legged sacks of meat and blood and bone dependent on the whole living planet for our survival. Our out breathings still flow through the pores of trees; our food still grows in dirt, our bodies decay. Of course, we all nod our heads in agreement. The gospel of ecology has become an intellectual commonplace. But it is not yet an emotional one. For most of us, most of the time, nature appears framed in a window or a video screen or inside the borders of a photograph. We do not feel the organic web passing through our guts, as it truly does. While our theories of nature have become wiser, our experience of nature has become shallower. And true fiction operates at a level deeper than shared intellectual slogans. Thus, any writer who sees the world in ecological perspective faces a hard problem: how, despite the perfection of our technological boxes, to make us feel the ache and tug of that organic web passing through us, how to situate the lives of characters—and therefore of readers—in nature.

Scott Russell Sanders appeals the writers should not limit writing to the human enclosures but to study the green world. Our age needs a revolution of vision which will enhance the standard of human life. Environment shapes every human gesture. The nature writing most engaged and forward looking will help us create a sustainable society.

Cynthia Deitering wrote, "The Postnatural Novel: The Toxic Consciousness in Fiction of the 1980s." He points out that fiction of the 1980s gives sustained and various representations of pollution. He proposes that recent American fiction reflects a 'toxic consciousness.' It offers an insight into a culture's shifting relation to nature and environment. Contemporary world has been facing the problem of ecological collapse. Deitering has provided a brief survey of American fiction and its preoccupation with the ecological collapse of the planet which British novelist Martin Amis has called "toiletisation of the planet." Concern with chemical contamination became one of the important themes in the novels written by the mid-1980s, the texts such as Don DeLillo's *White Noise*, Walker Percy's *The Thanatos Syndrome*, Paul Theroux's *O-Zone*, T. Coraghessan Boyle's *World's End*, and Richard Russo's *Mohawk*. Toxic waste functions as a cultural metaphor in recent fiction, which is the expression of a society's most general fears about its collective future. It is also an expression of an ontological rupture in its perception of the real.

'Toxic consciousness' in fiction reflects a fundamental shift in historical consciousness; people perceived a difference in their relation to the natural world and the ecosystems which are the foundations of all life forms. In post-industrial society people perceive a personal responsibility and national responsibility to the ecosystems. Cynthia Deitering asserts that people during the 1980s perceived that they are the inhabitants of a culture defined by its waste. A number of novels written during this period reflect the ontological alteration. She illustrated the point through two novels, Don DeLillo's *White Noise* and John Updike's *Rabbit at Rest*. Don DeLillo in the *White Noise* describes a society whose most conspicuous feature is its waste. He also dealt with the effects of consumer capitalism on the lives of the people. In consumer capitalism Gladney finds his identity in commodity products. He finds himself one in the configuration of waste products. He uses language which connects his identity to the commodities. The tract of land is now represented as a possible site of contaminated waste.

Rabbit Angstrom is the protagonist in John Updike's novel *Rabbit at Rest*. Rabbit is heart-frail. He is in a state of physical decay. He perceives the process of decay in the objects, the people, and the landscape around him. Human enterprises have subsumed nature in the urban locations. Fiction mirrors the society. Deitering calls the novels dealing with "toxic consciousness" as political texts. They provide a representation of a Postnatural world. It shows a culture defined by its waste. It shows the nations which has fouled its own nest. These novels raise the environmental consciousness of the people; people find the reflection of their own life in these novels. Pollution of natural world is represented in these novels.

Nineteenth century novels construct nature as a spiritual healer of the society. Twentieth century novels mirror the society which valued nature as an economic resource. The most recent fiction depicts a society which is living in Postnatural world. Nature is the life sustaining force surrounding mother earth.

Dana Phillips wrote the influential essay, "Is Nature Necessary?" He proposes that whether people admit it or not Nature plays an important role in shaping culture by its conspicuous presence or absence. Florida landscape is famous for Disney World, condos, shopping malls, golf courses. Florida exemplifies the changed relationship of the people in the landscape they inhabit. Dana Phillips points out that postmodern experience is irrelevant in the rural areas of the nation. People feel alienation from nature in urban centers. Interaction with nature is an essential characteristic feature of human progress.

Phillips argues that we cannot get solace in the absence of nature. The self is formed and invaded by nature. Postmodern experience is a collective category. He said that people in the contemporary period have misunderstood the role of nature in the human lives. Culture has subsumed nature. He expressed the hope that the inclusive political practice can survive and waken nature from its culturally induced coma. The eccentric hero Nick Adams in *Double Whammy* is the representative of the decentred and distorted social fabric he abhors.

Dana Phillips argues that we cannot dispense with nature altogether. The present-day politics is more demographic than democratic. He asserts that a politics with environmental goals can restore nature and culture both. Or the conditions mark the emergence of what seems to be a post political and thoroughly unnatural age. Postmodernism is the result of the epistemological basis of not only of the human relationship to nature, but of human relationships altogether. Freedom is false in postmodern age as it is constrained by a narrow range of options. The darker aspect of the postmodern age is the moment of a radical eclipse of the nature itself as Jameson suggested.

Nature has been dictating a new worldview of its own. We have had a great reverence for nature in the past. We ought to begin what Jameson has called "the practical reconquest of a sense of place." The forester and the forest are subsumed in the new form of social and natural organization. For bringing nature into culture, we must introduce necessary changes in the social and cultural fabric of the society. Ecological thinking necessitates a regard for totalities. The critics such as Wendell Berry, Heidegger, Debord, and Jameson distrust contemporary culture. Poet, novelist, essayist and farmer argue that global solutions to the problems of natural recovery cannot succeed. He insists that localities all around the globe must be involved in the effort to heal nature. Berry argued that nature is necessary because nature itself is necessity. Nature and human beings are interdependent. He argues that soil is our heritage, our history. That is the soil is also to be read, interpreted, taught, learned from, handed down to the next generation, and kept from becoming mere dirt. For Berry, farming is the conscious but controlled process of revolving nature into culture—and culture into nature. Attempts have been made in different parts of the world for the restoration of rivers to their natural state. Their condition was deteriorated to the level of a drainage canal. It is the symbol of cultural diagnosis. We must devote our cultural energy to coping with the negative effects of past policy decisions and actions. Past success stories are today's environmental disasters. Dana Phillips argues that we must convert the past mistakes into present sustainable development by thinking or working our way through the past. He states that we must realize the hope for revival or restoration of nature.

Glen A. Love wrote the seminal essay, "Revaluing Nature: Toward an Ecological Criticism." She referred to the writing of English historian, Arnold Toynbee who published the narrative history of the world in *Mankind and Mother Earth*. He pointed out the suicidal result of human action on the planet earth. He called for the prompt and vigorous actions to keep the earth a habitable place. He has listed the potential threats to the earth. Nuclear holocaust, radiation poisoning, chemical or germ warfare, alarming growth of the world's population are the potential threats to human life on earth evidences of global warming, destruction of the protective ozone layer, Disregard to nature has resulted into harmful effects of acid rain, cutting of the great forests, the critical loss of topsoil and groundwater, increasing rate of extinction plant and animal species. There are profound threats to our biological survival. We must stop keeping self-interest above the public interest irrationally enough in matters of common survival.

Glen A. Love considers that society as a whole and literary professionals have faced three crises in the last thirty years: civil rights, women's liberation, and environmental degradation. These problems have become world issues. Race, class, and gender are the issues with which much literary writing is preoccupied. We must acknowledge our place within the natural world. We have grown accustomed to living with crises. We must not depend on the past problem-solving strategies. The issue of degradation of earth has occupied a prominent place in English literature.

Joseph Meeker expresses a deep concern for nature in his seminal book *The Comedy of Survival: Studies in Literary Ecology* published in 1974. Meeker wrote:

> Human beings are the earth's only literary creatures.... If the creation of literature is an important characteristic of the human species, it should be examined carefully and honestly to discover its influence upon human behaviour and the natural environment—to determine what role if any it plays in the welfare and survival of mankind and what insight it offers into human relationships with other species and with the world around us. Is it an activity which adapts us better to the world or one which estranges us from it? From the unforgiving perspective of evolution and natural selection, does literature contribute more to our survival than it does to our extinction? (*The Comedy of Survival*, pp. 3-4)[14]

Meeker has presented the rereading of tragedy and comedy from an ecological perspective. The question of the rights of non-human organisms has become a vital concern in many disciplines. Ecological thinking has assumed a central place in central public policy. Environment has influenced religion, philosophy, law, history, anthropology, etc. It has also affected architecture and urban planning. Literary theory and criticism has not remained unaffected or unwilling to address which are at the forefront of public concern. Literary representations of Man's relationship with nature both influence and is influenced by that relationship. Glen A. Love argues that a nature-oriented literature corrects limited vision of the people; it offers a regard for the nonhuman life. Eco-consciousness rather than ego-consciousness is the need of the time in all spheres of life. Hemingway has profoundly dealt with the issue of ecology and non-human life. Anthropocentric misunderstand that natural literature is irrelevant and inconsequential. They mistook that nature is dull and unexciting while society is fascinating and refined. Modern ecology has made it clear that the greatest of all intellectual puzzles is the earth and the myriad systems of life which it nourishes. Nature reveals complex adaptive strategies which human mind could not devise. Nature can only teach the lessons of simplicity.

Glen A. Love asks for the redefinition of the pastoral in terms of the new and more complex understanding of nature as pastoral sense reflects the same sort of anthropocentric assumptions which are in dire need of reassessment. Man is a part of nature. She points out that the whole culture seems to follow an ecologically suicidal path. Freud, in *Civilisation and its Discontents,* Erich Froom in *The Sane Society*, and Paul Shepard in *Nature and Madness*, considered the question whether a society itself can be sick. They have arrived at the conclusion that a society can be sick.

Anthropologist writer Richard Nelson revealed that elevation of a person and place depends on the interaction between the two factors, place and people. He pointed out that our technological world has already begun to crack beneath our feet. He has told that, "our task is not to remake nature so that it is fit for humankind, but as Thoreau says to make humankind right for nature." Human beings should recognize their obligation to the shared natural world. Our survival in future depends on our acknowledgement of the contact with the green world. Many contemporary writers have shown a more radical awareness of the power of nature which rebuffs society's assumptions of control. Nature says, "I am here still, at the bottom of things, warming the roots of life; you cannot starve me nor tame me nor thwart me; I made the world, I rule it, I am its destiny" (*The Kingdom of Art*, 95). Literature which recognises and dramatises the integration of human with nature has been getting a widespread appeal. Critical theory which had gone further from the public life has got a redirection in the form of ecocriticism which asks elemental questions of ourselves.

Western American literature is not unique in its ecological perspective. Writers in England, Canada, Europe, South and Central America, Africa, Australia have been writing literary texts with ecological perspective. Consciousness and language are the prime concerns of literature; therefore we cannot be aloof from nature. Glen A. Love has stated the function of literature rightly: The most function of literature today is to redirect human consciousness to a full consideration of its place in a threatened natural world. Why does nature writing, literature of place, regional writing, poetry of nature, flourish now-even as it is ignored or denigrated by most contemporary criticism? Because of a widely shared sense—outside the literary establishment—that the current ideology which separates human beings from their environment is demonstrably and dangerously reductionist. The natural world is undoubtedly real and beautiful and significant.

We must recognize the primacy of nature. We should form a new ethic and aesthetics which embraces the human and the natural concerns. Paula Gunn Allen characterises some distinctive ways of perceiving reality and some fundamental assumptions about the universe of American Indians and its reflection in literature in "The Sacred Hoop: A Contemporary Perspective." She points out that the tribal people experience basic assumptions about the universe and the reality differently than the western people. The tribes seek to explore the dynamic aspect of life through song, ceremony, legend, sacred stories and tales. They regard nature as fundamental and sacred spring of life. They acknowledge the essential harmony of all things and see the equal value of all things. In tribal systems relationship is central. The American Indian sees all creatures as children of the mother earth. Indians conceive a circular, dynamic universe in which all things are related and are of one family. Ceremony and myth are the basic forms to American Indian literature. All ceremonies, whether for war or healing, create and support the sense of community, which is the bedrock of life. The community for tribes is not made up of only of the members of the tribe. It necessarily includes all beings that live in the tribe's universe. The American Indian literature is dynamic. The structures express and imply the relationship between human and non-human beings. The purpose of a ceremony is to integrate the individual with his or her fellows. The process expands individual consciousness. The person is restored to conscious harmony with the universe. The tribal people perceive things not as inert but as viable and alive and since all that is alive must grow and change; all existence can be manipulated under certain conditions and according to certain laws. The Indian is actually close to the earth.

Allen argues that the basic purpose of any culture is to maintain the ideal status quo. The basic assumptions about the nature of life and humanity's place in it play a pivotal role in the formation of culture. Peace, prosperity, good health, and stability are the paradigms of ideal status quo.

Ceremonial literature is sacred. It has power. It has a language of its own. The ceremonials restore the psychic unity of the people. Allen arrives at the conclusion that American Indian literature is rich, complex and express true meaning of people's lives. It teaches the respect for all life forms. Literature must express and articulate the deepest perceptions, relationships, and attitudes of a culture, whether it does so deliberately or accidentally. Tribal literature does this clearly without show. American Indian literature expresses the harmony of the universe and the community. The sense of unity among all things reflects in the songs and stories like a clear stream:

> There are birds of many colours—red, blue, green, yellow—yet it is all one bird. There are horses of many colours—brown, black, yellow and white—yet it is all one horse. So cattle, so all living things—animals, flowers, trees. So men: in this land where once were only Indians are now men of every colour—white, black, yellow, red—yet all one people. That this should come to pass was in the heart of the Great Mystery. It is right thus. And everywhere there shall be peace.[15]

The tribal people have the primary assumption that all things are of equal value in the scheme of things. The concept of being that is the fundamental spring of life finds finest articulation in the tribal literature. Leslie Marmon Silko, herself a Laguna Pueblo storyteller writes in "Landscape, History, and the Pueblo Imagination" describes pueblo people and their relationship to the land of the American Southwest. Pueblo oral narratives explain the world, helps people survive in it, and to transmit culture.

Interrelationships in pueblo landscape are multifaceted and delicate. Survival depended upon harmony and cooperation not only among human beings, but among all things—the animate and the less animate, rocks and mountains. Pueblo oral narratives illuminate that greed even the part of one being threatens the survival of all life on earth. Ancient pueblo people maintained and survived their culture through the oral tradition. Story telling was an important aspect of the culture. Location or place nearly always plays a central role in pueblo oral narratives. Ancient pueblo people could not conceive of themselves without a specific landscape. Location or setting is very important in pueblo narration of the stories.

Survival in any landscape depends on the best use of all available resources. Pueblo people believe that human beings are not separate from the natural world. Pueblo culture teaches people that we must respect and love the earth. Nature nurtures the spirituality of the people. They are grateful to the landscape because it helps them in their quest as spiritual people.

The ancient pueblo people had inclusive vision of the world. They strongly felt to leave nothing out. Pueblo oral tradition embraced all levels of human experience. They respected and loved the earth. They were grateful to the landscape. Landscape helped them for spiritualizing their lives.

In "A Taxonomy of Nature Writing", Thomas J. Lyon describes the nature of classification scheme of American nature literature. He points out three main dimensions of the literature of nature: natural history information, personal responses to nature, and philosophical interpretation of nature. John Hay in *Spirit of Survival* (1974) gives life histories of terns wonderfully, also provides the beauty and vulnerability of life itself. Rachel Carson in *The Sea around Us* (1950, 1961) arranges the facts of oceanography and marine biology. She has presented a holistic, ecological view of nature. William O. Pruitt put forth the theme of relationship through Animals of the north. Human beings' connection with nature is deep. Nature writing conveys a sense of wonder.

Michael Branch's "Indexing American Possibilities: The Natural History Writing of Bartram, Wilson, and Audubon" reviews the work of botanist William Bartram, ornithologist Alexander Wilson, and painter John James Audubon. He suggested that it is inaccurate to consider Henry David Thoreau the progenitor of American nature writing. Thoreau is the direct heir to the early romantic natural historians. We must recognize their contributions.

Nature is an expression of the divinity. The early romantic connection between human and non-human nature also helped to nurture the rise of natural history studies in America. Natural history functioned as an expression of America's need to discover the means by which its national destiny would be enacted. National faith is based upon the wilderness. The national literature is best expressed in terms of natural literature. Michael Branch argues: Americans demanded a culture that would be commensurate with the greatness of the land: as expansive as its prairies, as lofty as its mountains, as prolific as its forests. In short, natural history functioned as an expression of America's need to discover the means by which its national destiny would be enacted.

Wilderness itself inspires culture. Rich culture flourishes in the context of rich nature. Culture is associated with the land. Nature nurtures the culture. Wilderness is both a natural and cultural resource. Bartram, Wilson, and Audubon introduced a pattern of ecological thinking in American culture.

Travels is a landmark accomplishment in American literature. Bertram discovered and described a variety of species. His description is spontaneous and sincere. Coleridge called it a holy book. Bertram had a devout faith in the divinity of nature. He has opened the way for the spiritual resources of the wilderness. He reveals and celebrates the fabric of interrelationship that he recognised in the wilderness. He was sensitive to interconnectedness. He advocates nature through his writings. He suggested a respect for the dignity of all nature. He powerfully expresses the romantic belief that divinity is diffused throughout nature. He prefigured the "ecocentric egalitarianism" Alexander Wilson was America's foremost authority on birds. His monumental work is *American Ornithology.* He assumed very deliberately that his natural history was a contribution not only to science, but to the cultural identity of the nation. Fabric of nature crucially determines crucially determines the evolving national character of any nation. Wilson criticized the indefatigable human urge to destroy nature regardless of the consequences. Audubon suggested that the government should actively preserve the nature. He expressed concern for disappearing wilderness through his painting and poetry. He lamented the needless cruelty of man towards his fellow creatures. He was inspired by the divine beauty of nature. Thoreau read Audubon "with a thrill of delight". William Bertram, Alexander Wilson, and John James Audubon make clear that early romantic literature is an essential source of the American nature writing tradition. They indexed the possibilities for American culture in the fecund wilderness of the New World. They relocated divinity from ecclesiastical institutions to the natural landscape and its non-human institutions. They celebrated their kinship with nature.

Don Scheese in "Desert Solitaire: Counter Friction to the Machine in the Garden" considers one of Thoreau's most colourful followers, Edward Abbey. Edward Abbey, John Muir, Aldo Leopold, all of whom sought to instill a land ethic in the American public. Scheese admits that he was highly influenced by Edward Abbey's *Desert Solitaire*. He studied the nature writing tradition. D.H. Lawrence wrote in *Studies in Classic American Literature*: Edward Abbey is a nature writer like Thoreau, John Muir, and Aldo Leopold. D.H. Lawrence writes: "The few such writers whom I wholly admire are those like Thoreau, who went far beyond simple nature writing to become the critics of society, of the state, of our modern industrial culture.... It is not enough to understand nature; the point is to save it." Edward Abbey like Thoreau, Muir and Leopold was an exemplary inhabitor of the wild. He celebrated the harsh beauty of the desert landscape. He articulated new arguments, distinguished by rhetoric of rage, for wilderness preservation. He advocated political activism in order to defend wild nature. Since the publication of *Desert Solitaire* nature writing and environmental politics have been significantly transformed. Don Scheese emphasises that, "Abbey's life has become a counter friction against those forces that would destroy the wilderness." Mary Austin in *The Land of Little Rain* (1903) dealt with the harmonious adaptations of animals and Indians to sparse resources, to understand the rhythm of the land; one must dwell on it for a significant period of time, and the careless exploitation of natural resources by Anglo Americans. An art critic, Van Dyke emphasized the aesthetic value of desert landforms.

In *Desert Solitaire,* Edward Abbey has written about the integrity, stability, and beauty of the desert. He has presented a biocentric outlook. Edward Abbey and Aldo Leopold have expressed the deep concern for the preservation of the land, its harmony, and the equilibrium of the landscape. Abbey proposed that the root of our ecological crisis is cultural: "Our country is not being destroyed [merely] by bad politics, it is being destroyed by a bad way of life." Abbey and Marx have advanced the cause of biocentrism and deep ecology. Abbey meditates: "wilderness is not a luxury but a necessity of the human spirit, and as vital to our lives as water and good bread."

Thoreau has observed that the most important value of wildness is spiritual. Spiritual recreation takes place in the wildness. Muir reiterated Thoreau's belief in the spiritual value of wilderness. Leopold in *Sand Country Almanac* said that nature nurtures aesthetic, spiritual and recreational value of the wild. Edward Abbey has brought out the preservation of the wild is essential for the political reasons also. It is a safe haven for revolutionaries from authoritarian government. He has cited the examples of Vietnam, Cuba, and Algeria. Wilderness was a foundation for guerrillas to mount effective resistance to dictatorial regimes. In order to recreate oneself, one should immerse in nature. In the beginning of the twentieth century people realized the importance of "Back to Nature". "Back to Wilderness" movement surfaced in 1960s and 1970s.

Veral L. Norwood explores the difference between masculine and feminine environmental ethics in "Heroines of Nature: Four Women Respond to the American Landscape." Women writers have made significant contribution to our understanding of the environment. She examines four women nature writers: Isabella Bird, Mary Austin, Rachel Carson and Anny Dillard. Natural environment is central to culture in every nation of the world. In *The Death of Nature*, Carolyn Merchant implies that women's movement and ecology movement started on around the same beliefs that have dominated western culture since the scientific revolution:

> Both the women's movement and the ecology movement are sharply critical of the costs of competition, aggression, and domination arising from the market economy's modus operandi in nature and society.[16] (*The Death of Nature*, p. xvi)

Isabella Bird wrote her experiences of nature in "A Lady's Life in the Rocky Mountains." She sought a denial of the weakness of self in the wilderness. She determined to visit Rockies for religious solitude. She discovers herself in nature.

She comes to a better understanding of her place in the world. She sought a transcendental experience in nature. It has taken her beyond herself and into contemplation of God. She realized that there is the need to simplify one's life in order to focus on higher questions. Nature raises grandeur and sublimity of life. Nature improves the beholder morally, spiritually, intellectually, and aesthetically. She abhors the development of the natural landscape by American entrepreneurs. She finds inspiration in the mountains.

Mary Austin supremely concerns with the relationship between the geologic and the biophysical landscape. She seeks to resolve the conflict between nature and culture. In her most famous book *The Land of Little Rain,* she explicates the possibility for responsible, civilized life in the wilderness landscape. She expressed concern for misrepresentation of nature, particularly wilderness nature in the Anglo western culture. Austin values all life in the desert. *The Land of Little Rain* offers the interesting account of the interacting physical and biological landscape of the desert southwest. She found beauty in the desolate colours of the desert. A land forces new habits on its dwellers. Mary Austin observes that one does not understand person until one has lived in the place from which they spring.

Rachel Carson condemned the life-destroying potential of pesticides in her classic *Silent Spring*. She got National Book Award for *The Sea Around Us*. In her acceptance speech for the National Book Award for *The Sea around Us,* why her book became so popular, which has little to say directly about human life. She has explored impact of landscape on the human life: "The materials of science are the materials of life itself. Science is part of the reality of living; it is the what, the how and the why of everything in our experience. It is impossible to understand man without understanding his environment and the forces that molded him physically and mentally."

Carson explicates that there is an organic, interactive connection between humans and the rest of the biosphere. *The Sea Around Us* details the discoveries new scientific technology has made possible. It reveals a deep concern with the hubris attached to discovery. It critiques the historical inability of people to take the long view of their actions in respect to nature. Carson laments the destruction of wild landscapes. She defines the causes with precision and concern. She meditated on the destructive impact civilization had on the environment. The growth of civilization destroys the environment. The increased knowledge only can stop the destruction of the nature.

Carson criticizes the use of oceans as dump for radioactive wastes. She points out that radioactive waste can have disastrous impacts both on ocean life and life on land. She suggests that we should maintain a proper respect for the environment that gave us life. Wilderness continues as both threat and promise. The choice between garden and desert was an issue in 1960 as live as it had been in 1660.

Annie Dillard provides a classic vision of landscape in *Pilgrim at Tinker Creek*. She is concerned with the individual, personal relationships to God, and nature. She is a master of natural description. She knows her place intimately. One who understands the Tinker Creek may easily understand the rest of the world. She meditates upon the beauty and horror of and in creation. She finds beauty equally in the grand and simple aspects. Dillard challenges the hubris that would place culture as a construct above nature. She rejects duality between nature and culture. Nature and culture are not two opposite things. They are complimentary to each other. She prioritises nature above culture. Dillard proposes that human culture is but one aspect of nature. Culture is a way of response to nature. The understanding of nature might better the human culture. Immersion of self into nature sublimates life.

Scott Slovic wrote an insightful essay, "Nature Writing and Environmental Psychology: The Interiority of Outdoor Experience." The very mystery of nature contributes to the independence and self-awareness of the observer. One must deepen one's respect and understanding for nature. All contemporary American nature investigates the relationship between nature and the human mind. He meditates on nature or the interaction between man and nature. He has presented natural experience—the heightened and dulled awareness of nature. Abbey presents a green-beret turned ecoterrorist in *The Monkey Wrench Gang*. His most famous work of non-fiction *Desert Solitaire* is an elegy for the fast disappearing pristine of country. *The Monkey Wrench Gang* is a straightforward call to arms for environmentalists and radical preservationist groups as Earth First! Environmentalists call it as their bible. Scott Slovic considers The Monkey Wrench the Lolita of the environmental movement. Abbey's novel heightens our attentiveness to the issues of the environment. We must revitalize our connection to nature. For Berry awareness or watchfulness is indeed an exalted state of mind. Through prolonged contact with nature one may understand the mystery of the place and nature but one must be watchful. Berry reflects on the connection between the self and nature.

Slovic observes that recent nature writing effects concrete changes in the readers' attitudes towards the environment. It inspires environmentally sound behaviour. Awareness of the environment is a necessary. Cheryll Burgess [Glotfelty] in the paper entitled "Toward an Ecological Criticism" argues that it is the responsibility of critics and teachers to point out the environmental implications of literary texts, to engage in "ecocriticism."

Barry Lopez explains in *The Arctic Dreams* a deeper understanding of nature is a prerequisite for the enlightened human activities. He asserts that the goal of the writer is to nourish the awareness of the readers. He shows a sense of deep respect for the place. The surge of environmental consciousness occurred during the 1960s and 1970s. The environment literature makes us aware that there is the urgent need that we must act respectfully and responsibly to nature. Nature Writing is a literature of hope. It is assumed that elevation of consciousness may lead to wholesome political change. Scott Slovic concludes: "Natural literature is concerned perhaps primarily with the interior landscape, with the mind itself."

Michael J. McDowell in "The Bakhtinian Road to Ecological Insight" considers what critical approach seems most promising for an ecological analysis of landscape writing. He argues the Russian philosopher and a literary critic Mikhail Bakhtin's literary theory gives an ideal point of view for ecocritics. Landscape literature critiques the values of progress, development and improvement celebrated by a dominant tradition. Landscape writing in America has questioned the values of progress, development and improvement. Systems and relationships are important in the phenomenal world. Philip Slater said in *The Pursuit of Loneliness* that alternatives that are opposing to dominant emphases of a social system caution the social change. McDowell argues that a holistic world view is more compatible with the ecological discoveries of the past thirty than Cartesian dualism. He observes that literary studies have been slow to abandon the nineteenth-century certainty to literature such as New Criticism. New Criticism closely analyses a work of art as an object in itself. Many recent postmodernist critical theories have been exclusively concerned with the analysis of language. These theories ignored physical world, though they have not outrightly rejected its importance. History, philosophy, anthropology and other soft disciplines have long provided a ground upon which a critic can stand to lift the world of literature. Russian philosopher and critic, Mikhail Bakhtin has integrated into his theories systems and relationships embraced by the hard sciences.

Bakhtin's theory explores the science of relationships. McDowell considers that Bakhtin's theories provide an ideal. According to Bakhtin, the ideal form to represent reality is a dialogical form. In the dialogical form there is the communication of multiple voices or points of view. Ecological literary criticism explores the interaction of both the human and non-human. According to Bakhtin, a dialogical form is the ideal form to represent reality. In dialogical form multiple voices or points of view interact. Writers employ various strategies such as authorial speech, inserted genres, and the speech of the characters to express interplay of various socio-ideological positions. Monological form encourages singular speaking subject. It suppresses whatever does not fit his or her ideology. All entities in the web of nature deserve recognition and voice. An ecological literary criticism explores how authors have represented the relations of both the human and non-human voices in the landscape. We must suppress our ego, to achieve union with nature. Fromm rightly implies objectivity is an illusion. McDowell asks us to acknowledge and celebrate the crediting of natural objects with human qualities. Ecocritics analyse writer's perception of the landscape, mountains, and animals' relationship with other parts of the landscape and with humans. We must acknowledge and celebrate Ruskin's "pathetic fallacy" the crediting of natural objects with human qualities. Pathetic fallacy is not the romantic illusion. It is an inevitable component of human perception.

Dialogics can be applied to landscape literature that enhances an analysis of ecological relationships among all the landscape's components including humans. It emphasises contradictory voices, rather than dealing only with the monologic voice. Characters and elements of landscape influence each other. Bakhtin has rightly said that all meaning is determined by the context of an utterance. Bakhtin proposed that every creature defines itself. Every creature becomes 'self' mentally, spiritually, and physically by its interaction with other beings and things. William Blake said, "Without contraries is no progression." Context includes all earlier texts as well as the great multiplicity of contemporary voices and even those of the future. The landscape writing exhibits the characteristic which Bakhtin calls 'open-endedness.' It indicates the door continually open for dialogue. Recently writers have been expressing a strong sense of place through their writing. Writers associate human characters with the elements of landscape.

Dialogical analysis of landscape literature explicates ecological relationships among all the landscape's components, including humans. It emphasises contradictory voices rather than focusing mainly upon the authoritative monologic voice of the narrator. Characters and elements of landscape influence each other. Landscape writing demonstrates the value of "open-endedness."

Bakhtin's concept of the *chronotope* expresses the inseparability of time and space. Chronotope is a twentieth century neologism. It combines time and space. Interconnection of time and space is artistically expressed in literature. The twentieth century neologism combines *chronos* (time) and *topos* (place) which Bakhtin defines as "the intrinsic connectedness of temporal and spatial relationships that are artistically expressed in literature." It expresses the inseparability of space and time. Chronotope recovers the representation of place in literature. It binds together the elements of story, geography and self. Human life is conjoined with the life of nature.

Psychologists tell us that memory of a person can function well when he/she has a strong sense of place. One's taste, ideas, and values are shaped in some extent by the places where one lives. Neil Evernden suggests that we are deluding ourselves when we speak as if we have no environmental context. Landscape is not just a collection of physical forms. The story, geography, and self are inextricably bound together (Evernden, 19).

Bakhtin observes that with the rise of capitalism novelists addressed the problems of how a person must fit into a bourgeois society. Thoreau, Jeffers, and Silko have made plural, diverse and more accurate representation of nature through their writing. Human integration into the landscape is presented by many novelists and poets. Many novelists have made the landscape famous through their creative writing; Thomas Hardy popularized Wessex, D.H. Lawrence wrote about the Midlands, Cheryll Burgess [Glotfelty] uses Elaine Showalter's model of the stages through which feminist criticism has progressed. It describes analogous phases through which ecological criticism has been moving. Burgess [Glotfelty] presents a very accurate and useful typology of ecological literary criticism. It raises our consciousness of stereotypes, distortions, and omissions of the representations of nature in literature. The second kind of criticism recognizes or rediscovers the tradition of nature writing in both neglected and celebrated writers. The third kind of criticism is theoretical, which would include the discussion of deep ecology, Ecofeminism, and ecological poetics.

Joseph Meeker mixed the literary and environmental interests. According to him literature contributes more to our survival than extinction. Literary form must be reconciled with the form and structure of nature. Both the nature and literary forms are related to human perception of beauty and balance. Henry David Thoreau, Robinson Jeffers, Barry Lopez, Annie Dillard, and Leslie Silko have achieved synthesis of literary forms and nature.

Some ecological literary critics condemn western civilization for its oppression of nature. They often find environmental concerns in Eastern thought or the religious attitudes of the primitive people. Western tradition too accommodated the contradictory things. Non-western thought of nature has influenced the mainstream thought of the western culture. Ecocriticism attempts a radical critique of dominant western attitudes. But it is not a wholesale rejection in favour of a stereotyped and polarized alternative system. One of the important concerns of ecocriticism is stylistics. How does the writer represent landscape through metaphor? The ecocritics analyse how the writer has modified existing genres for an understanding of the complex relationships within nature. Views of humanity in nature have influenced contemporary literature.

Practical Ecocriticism

Practical Ecocriticism deals with the methods the landscape writers have used to enable a dialogical interplay of voices and values. Michael J. McDowell makes an important assumption that 'environment creates a character or characters, so that the study of the environment with which a character interacts will reveal much about the character. He ponders: "An exploration of the dialogic voice in a landscape leads naturally to an analysis of the values a writer has recognised as inherent in a landscape rather than imposed upon it." Ecocriticism recognizes an integral relationship between value and landscape. Susan Griffin illustrates in *Woman and Nature: The Roaring Inside Her*: "Impersonal, seemingly objective representations of reality are usually the product of our dominant ideology, whose greatest success is its invisibility as an ideology."

Attitudes often determine the relationships. Columbus' perception of the New World was based upon the utility value of landscape in the form of gold and persons in the form of servants. Such view persisted for half a millennium. This view created an exploitative relationship between humans and nature.

Writers recognize values in a landscape. McDowell suggests a closer understanding of the elements of the landscape. He explicated the ways in which the writers use place to establish meaning. The writers who deal with landscape emphasize the sense of place. Narratives are often organically rooted. Environment plays as important role as the characters and narrators in the novel.

Ecocriticism also concerns with the limits of each writer's views. McDowell asks us to understand the importance of "a blank spot on the map." He concludes essay with Bakhtin's view of the texts: "For every text is a dialogue open for further comments from other points of view. There is no conclusion."

Ethics are implicated in the way we talk about the world, the way we perceive it. We must have the courage to learn the language of nature to reanimate nature. Our language should be free from an obsession with human pre-eminence. We should follow the path of ontological humility and egalitarianism. We must re-establish the communication with nature.

REFERENCES

1. Worster, Donald. *The Wealth of Nature: Environmental History and the Ecological Imagination*. New York: Oxford University Press, 1993.
2. Duerr, Hans Peter. *Dreamtime: Concerning the Boundary Between Wilderness and Civilisation*. Trans. Goodman Felicitas. Oxford: Basil Blackwell, 1985.
3. Evernden, Neil. *The Natural Alien: Humankind and Environment*. Toronto: University of Toronto Press, 1985.
4. Lukacs, George. *History and Class Consciousness*. Trans. Rodney Livingstone. Cambridge: MIT Press, 1968.
5. Foucault, Michel. *Madness and Civilisation*. Trans. Richard Howard. New York: Vintage, 1973.
6. Duerr, Hans Peter. *Dreamtime: Concerning the Boundary Between Wilderness and Civilisation*. Trans. Felicitas Goodman. Oxford: Basil Blackwell, 1985.

7. Foucault, Michel. "Politics, Philosophy, Culture: Interviews and other Writings". trans. Alan Sheridan. New York: Routledge, 1988.
8. Heidegger, Martin. *An Introduction to Metaphysics,* trans. Ralph Mannheim, New Haven, Conn.: Yale University Press, 1959.
9. Fromm, Harold. *The Nature of Being Human: From Environmentalism to Consciousness*. Baltimore: The Johns Hopkins University Press, 2009.
10. Page, La., Wilbur F., and Sally Ranney. "The Heart and Soul of Culture." *Changing Views on Controversial Environmental Issues*. ed. Theodore, D. Goldferb. Guilford, Conn: Dushkin Publishing Group, 1989.
11. Cobb, Edith. *The Ecology of Imagination in Childhood*. New York: Columbia University Press, 1977.
12. Shepard, Paul. "Ecology and Man—A Viewpoint." *The Subversive Science*. ed. P. Shepard and D. Mckinley. New York: Haughton Mifflin, 1969.
13. Rueckert, William. "Literature and Ecology." *The Ecocriticism Reader: Landmarks in Literary Ecology*. ed. Cheryll Glotfelty and Harold Fromm. Athens, Georgia: The University of Georgia Press, 1996.
14. Hansford, Charles. "My Country's Worth." *The Poems of Charles Hansford*. ed. James A. Servies and Carl R. Dolmetsch. Chapel Hill: University of North Carolina Press, 1961.
15. Meeker, Joseph. *The Comedy of Survival: Studies in Literary Ecology*. New York: Scribner's, 1972.
16. Merchant, Carolyn. *The Death of Nature: Women, Ecology and the Scientific Revolution*. New York: Harper Collins Publishers, 1990 (p. xvi).

3

Harold Fromm

Harold Fromm
The co-editor of The Ecocriticism Reader

Harold Fromm is a visiting scholar at the University of Arizona. He is widely known for his writings on self, the environment, and academia. He is the co-editor of *The Ecocriticism Reader* and the author of *Academic Capitalism and Literary Value.*

Fromm's *The Nature of Being Human* is a first-person account of the revelations of nature. Harold Fromm is a University Associate in English as well as a member of the Institute of the Environment at the University of Arizona in Tucson. His interests range from environmentalism, Darwinian evolution, to consciousness studies. Harold Fromm began writing on air pollution in 1970s. He co-edited with Cheryll Glotfelty, *The Ecocriticism Reader: Landmarks in Literary Ecology*. He reviewed books with humanistic and scientific perspective in *SCIENCE* magazine.

The physical relationship between the natural world and the individual is confirmed. There is the strong relationship between the surroundings in which we live and our power of creativity. Our idea of self and free will are determined by the natural influences. Ecocritic, Harold Fromm explores the relationship between human life and nature. He argues that our perceived separation from our surroundings is an illusory construct. His exploration is based on ecology, evolutionary psychology, and consciousness studies.

In the Gestalt Perspective, individual cannot exist alone. Each individual exists within an environmental field. He/she must engage with the surrounding to survive physically, he must be able to fulfill his basic needs by using the necessary resources from his surroundings. He/she must engage with persons in the environment to survive psychologically. Both the individual and the environment must be studied, described in the literary works.

In *The Nature of Being Human*, Fromm personalized ecocritical discourse. The book is a series of informative, persuasive and articulate essays. He acknowledges the relationship between human mind and natural environment. The Nature of Being Human is a lively and impressive book about the nature and human life interrelationships. Fromm expressed views on the physical quality of the air and its effects on people in chapter first, "Awakening to the Environment." He said that public must be aware of the environment. Physical quality of the air is of supreme importance for the psychic and physical health of an individual. The World Bank estimates that in China four lakh people died because of outdoor air pollution, three lakhs from indoor pollution, and sixty thousand from toxic water. He developed an argument for preservation of nature. His argument is based on Eastern and Western philosophy. A few people are aware of the effects of pollution upon one's own behaviour, mental sharpness, emotional states, and physical performance. The nature of the environment influences physical health, psychological health of the people.

Fromm observed a link between deteriorating environment and production of psychological states like excitement, depression, wounded self-esteem, and cheating, drugs, crime and other pathologies. He addressed the issue of the current environmental crises. The movement to save the environment is not as selfless and magnanimous as might at first appear. We are not doing a disinterested favour to the environment through the movement. The distinction between the environment and human life is illusory. Environment is one of the aspects of survival. Species survive or perish as a result of their compatibility with the environment of their time. We as individuals survive or perish because of our own personal compatibilities with our immediate life environments, which are aspects of the larger whole. Our very thoughts are linked to planetary conditions. Psychology, Marxism, feminism, Lacanianism, structuralism, postcolonialism and queer theories have exerted insightful influence on the literary scholarship. Ecocriticism has revitalized sense of the richness of both life and literature.

Human dispositions powerfully influence the products of the human imagination. In literature drama or narrative is more or less adaptive. Everything human ultimately derives from the evolved body and brain, Forms of expression may change on the basis of individual consciousness and culture.

Chapter two, "On Being Polluted" presents Harold Fromm's personal account of the awareness of pollution. He became aware of pollution for the first-time years ago when he was a graduate student at the University of Wisconsin. He says that pollution was too obvious to be missed in Gary. Pollution had been bearable but very unpleasant. Pollution causes burning eyes, curious oppressive headaches, and a general feeling of strangeness. Pollution is also responsible for distressing ailments: dizziness, nausea, tingling pains in the extremities, and lethargic aimlessness. It impairs our ability to read, concentrate, and to get things done.

The effects of pollution on daily lives have become greater all the time. Most people for one or the other reason are unaware most of the time of any actual pollution though they were aware intellectually of the existence of a problem. Pollution is ruining our lives. The people who are the natives of an industrial area are apparently insensitive to the existence of pollution. Living in the smokes for one's entire life make people part of the normal, unnoticed environment.

According to Fromm, second cause of the obliviousness of pollution is the fact that most of the people who live in the area where there is little pollution are unaware of the destructive effects of pollution on our lives. Fromm observed that the third cause of unawareness is the smoking of cigarettes and other tobacco. Smoker is not conscious of the effects of pollution. Smokers live in an ambience of smoke and smells therefore they are not very much aware of the outside world. Air pollution has tremendous effects on plants and people. The effects of air pollution on humans are dizziness, nausea, pains, headaches, burning eyes, lethargy, etc. In chapter second, Fromm addressed the connection of concrete material circumstances with the daily human life.

Chapter third "From Transcendence to Obsolescence" is a philosophical, reflective essay which explores the influence of nature on human life. Environmental movement has contributed to the public and private environmental awareness around the globe. This essay also played a role as a seminal precursor to the subjective realities of life. Pollution affects one's lifestyle and health in a great extent. The quality of the air influences one's day-to-day feelings.

There is a connection between weather and one's physical state. The weather affects one's mental state too. One could not survive without air. There is only one source of air-outside air. One feels miserable in the polluted air. Fromm explicated that air-conditioners and staying in-doors are not the remedies for pollution. Pollutants travel very far indeed.

Fromm pointed out that in the present time Nature is a great mystery for many people. It is not beyond their understanding. It is virtually non-existent to the perceptions of the average children. When Technology obscured physical nature at every point, psychological problems turn up later on in life.

Humankind failed to see that now, as in the past; the roots of its being are in the earth. In the past people understood the intimate connections of life in the earth, because the effects of nature on people's lives were immediate. Now our life is mediated by technology. People think that not nature but technology is actually responsible for everything in their life. The modern humanity has developed its own mythology of voluntary omnipotence. The myth is very apparent in the industrial corporations. They attack the very basic concept of environmental protection. Fromm said that the characteristic flaw of the tragic hero is conceited pride and a refusal to recognize his own finitude. The tragic flaw of the contemporary people is their unwillingness to recognize that nature is the support system for their life. Very few physicians are aware about psychological and physiological effects of pollution. Pollution makes people low spirited.

It is not merely genes, psychic history, parents, social class that determines one's accomplishments, moods and perspectives. It is also the nature that influences immediately on the lives of the people to a large extent. Pollution makes people irritable without irritants, pessimistic without philosophy, hungry without fasting, tired without having spent any energy, and afflicted with heartburn and indigestion without recent food.

Elements in the physical environment impact social behaviour. *The Times* emphasises the effects of positive ions on "people's mood and health, even precipitating suicides, crimes and accidents." Pollution also causes tension and irritability among the people.

Before two hundred years Boswell expressed his intuitive awareness of the concrete connection between nature and human life thorough his writing. In "Ecocriticism's Genesis" Fromm said that William Rueckert is usually cited as the true begetter of the term "ecoriticism." He used the word in his 1978 essay "Literature and Ecology: An Experiment in Ecocriticism." Fromm personally feels that the only true begetter of the term Ecocriticism is Cheryll Glotfelty (formerly Burgess). Cheryll Glotfelty with Fromm brought out the first and the best anthology on the nature writing and its practitioners.

Writing about environment is not entirely a new genre. One could trace it back to Eastern writing, and Theocritus, the Medievals, the European Enlightenment, the Romantics, the Transcendentalists. Association for the Study of Literature and Environment (ASLE) was established in the early 1990s. Interdisciplinary Study of Literature and Environment appeared in 1993. With the arrival of The Ecocriticism Reader in 1996, the situation changed rapidly. Ecocritism covers a broad spectrum. It serves as an umbrella term for very various activities. It is unwilling to be hijacked by a single, theoretical, fetishistic perspective.

Fromm proposes that environment matters in the social, philosophical, scientific, and political aspects of life.

Chapter fourth "Air and Being" deals with the influence of air on the human life. The influences of the air are irresistible. After Darwin, Marx, and Freud the sports ground of human freedom has come to seem painfully withered. We should recognize environmental constraints upon our behaviour. Fromm has narrated the personal experience of having lived in the dramatically polluted environment of north-west Indiana, not far from the steel mills and power plants that line the shores of Lake Michigan from Chicago to Michigan City. The most people are aware of pollution in the limited extent. The effects of air pollution on the general population are rarely discussed in the media.

There are few if any safe places that may protect people from the effects of pollution. Harold Fromm and Gloria Fromm moved from their rural farm fifteen miles south of Gary, Indiana, to their home about sixty miles northwest of Gary, Indiana. They changed the residence for the sole reason that the air was making them ill more than half the year. Chicago's northwest suburbs they experienced to be polluted though less in degree.

Mary Mellor rightly said, "Human-human relations are embedded in and constructed from human-nature relations." We should acknowledge that we are all part of an organic system. Insensitive policies endanger the ecosystem and threaten the very survival of human societies. Human life is inextricably linked with the nature. We should recognize humanity's kinship with the nature. Kamala Markandaya represented symbiosis between man and nature in *Nectar in a Sieve*. Nature nurtures human societies. It is an ever sustaining resource for all human development.

Chapter five is entitled as "Ecocriticism' Genesis." William Rueckert is usually cited as the only true begetter of the term "Ecocriticism" in his 1978 essay "Literature and Ecology: An Experiment in Ecocriticism." According to Cheryll Glotfelty ecological concerns are so pressing that they ought to eclipse every other concern. She completed her Ph.D. in American Literature at Cornell University. She finished up her dissertation on representations of nature in the American women's literary tradition. She said, "If I can't find a way to approach literature ecologically then, I will have to abandon this profession as frivolous." A new organization devoted to nature writing was established as the "Association for the Study of Literature and Environment." *The Ecocriticism Reader: Landmarks in Literary Ecology* inaugurated a new field of study, ecocriticism. Ecocriticism is today a bona fide field of study with unofficial headquarters at the University of Nevada, Reno, where Cheryll Glotfelty, Michael Branch, and Scott Slovic have pioneered a programme. In 1990, Cheryll became the first official Assistant Professor of Literature and the Environment.

Harold Fromm presented the effect of air pollution on the body and thence on consciousness. He gave an explicit account of environment/*body/mind* interaction. Nature writing is not completely a new genre of writing. One could find traces of nature writing in Theocritus, Plato, and Aristotle. Literature of the East is rich in nature writing. Ecocriticism covers a broad range. It is an umbrella term for very diverse activities. It has diverse perspectives as it deals with a broad spectrum.

Fromm expressed the view that ecocriticism has the potential to bring necessary developments in the arts, society and even international relations in an age of global warming. Consciousness like trees and pollution is one of the material products of the environment.

"Ecology and Ideology" is the title of chapter six. Many ideologies are in ruins today. A new intellectual universe called ecology has emerged for revitalizing inspired insights. People have been expressing concern for deforestation. People have become aware of chemical and nuclear disasters. We should restore the awareness of people's connectedness with the earth that produced them. Industrial Revolution made mankind appeared self-creating, autonomous, and omnipotent. Ecology has filtered through philosophy, sociology, ethics, political science, psychology, history, economics, legal studies, religion, literature, and literary criticism.

In "Ecology and Ideology" Fromm introduced revitalizing and inspired insights into a new intellectual movement known as Ecocriticism. People must acknowledge the age old awareness of people's connectedness with the material (earth) that produced them. The effect has been taking place after a long cessation during the Industrial Revolution made mankind seem self-creating, autonomous, and omnipotent. Ecology influenced considerably philosophy, ethics, sociology, political science, psychology, history, economics, legal studies, religion, and even literature and literary criticism. In the last twenty years ecological awareness has generated an intellectual upheaval which considers the impact of nature on all various aspects of life.

Ecological activities are not just concerned with "stop pollution". They have produced an ideology which defines nature, value, objectives of life on this planet. Dave Foreman's *Confessions of an Eco-Warrior* is an interesting account of social and philosophical relevance of environment. He expressed powerful emotions for the preservation of wilderness and biological diversity.

According to Harold Fromm unlike literary Marxism, feminism, and queer theory, ecocriticism will be around for a long time. It is able to shape itself to unexpected developments in the arts, society, and even international relationships in an age of global warming.

Dave Foreman and Murray Bookchin focused very bright light on one area of the ecological spectrum. Foreman worked for the Wilderness Society from 1973 to 1980. Tired of compromises with federal bureaucracy in 1980 he became one of founders of Earth First! The action group employed direct intervention to stop environmentally destructive development, deforestation, and dam building as well as road construction in wilderness areas. Foreman has expressed the principles and accomplishments of the action group in the *Confessions of an Eco-Warrior*. His account makes them appear, on balance, a positive force:

> We do not engage in radical action because we are primarily motivated by opposition to authority, because we are antinomians, but because we are for something—the beauty, wisdom, and abundance of this living planet.[1]

Foreman is averse to the politics of both the Left and the Right. He believed that ecological problems are more important than economic and social problems.

Murray Bookchin has been a passionate social activist like Foreman. He has written the magnum opus *The Ecology of Freedom*. He is at his best in *Remaking Society: Pathways to a Green Future*. He is the brilliant, mordant, racy, realistic, social philosopher. He is a utopian idealist. The Utopist focuses on the past and the future, the realist on the present. He has given the account of the non-hierarchical, no dominating families:

> It is hard for the modern mind to appreciate that precapitalist societies identified social excellence with cooperation rather than competition; disaccumulation rather accumulation; public service rather than private interest; the giving of gifts rather than the sale of commodities; and care and mutual aid rather than profit and rivalry.[2] (46-47)

Bookchin choreographs the falling off of this primal egalitarian society through stages involving acquisition of power, first by elders, then by males, warriors, small communities, city-states with direct representation, and family nation states with indirect or no representation, dominated by capitalist or communist power structures. This increase of chain of command, domination, and exploitation of each other is part and parcel of our supremacy of nature. It is hierarchy not anthropocentrism that is responsible for today's ecological devastation.

Bookchin observed that ecological problems are only one aspect of a system of social domination extending from the human being/nature relationship to the person/person relationship. In such relationships both people and nature are degraded into the role of "resources" for exploitation by those on top. Bookchin proposed that hierarchical power relations are at the heart of all forms of exploitation and oppression.

Bookchin is one of the most powerful critics of the contemporary society. He has analysed hypocrisy, self-deception, and destruction involved in capitalism and Marxism. The ruthless expansionist foundation of capitalism requires that more and more forests, minerals, animals, and people be used to produce more and more products.

Fromm observed that many people view that the problem of the environment is an unimportant arabesque drawn around the important concerns of human life. He proposes that the environmental problem must ultimately be seen as a central philosophic and ontological question about the self-definition of contemporary humanity. He emphasises that the human relationship with nature is consistent. Contemporary humankind's perspective towards is arrogant, shocking, and suicidal disregard of its roots in the earth. Natural influence on human life is irresistible. Most people are not aware of how pollution concretely affects them at every moment of life. Polluted air is bad for humanity, plants, and for animals. *Defending the Earth* came about in the late eighties. Bookchin explicated that the "ecological society" of the future would replace capitalism with a non-hierarchical "libertarian municipalism". The political power will be decentralized; the local communities would take care of the neighboring ecosystems. The community would be self-sufficient in energy and commodity. It would eliminate the use of non-renewable fossil fuels. It would end the domination over people and nature by the top levels of power structure. "Either we will turn to seemingly 'utopian' solutions based on decentralization, a new equilibrium with nature, and the harmonization of social relations, or we face the very real subversion of the material and natural basis for human life on the planet." Bookchin's

Defending the Earth provides compressed statements of the Bookchin's and Foreman's ideology. Both of them made the observation of the failure and inability of capitalism to deal ecological problems until they become terrible.

Ecological activities are not just related to stop pollution. They are the products of larger belief systems. Deep ecology, eco-feminism, and social ecology define the nature value, and ends of life on this planet. Ecology is also an ideology. Dave Foreman has written an interesting book, *Confessions of an Eco-Warrior*. Murray Bookchin has written Remaking Society.

Reform ecology sounds good but was not adequate for conservation of the environment. It is tinkering with the leading, capitalist, human-oriented, western mode of life that is destroying the planet. Many organizations like Natural Resources Defence Council, Environmental Action, the League of Conservation Voters, and the Sierra Club are dismissed by radicals as co-opted tools of industrialism and technology. They aim to change the path and pace but not the overall direction toward ecological destruction.

Deep ecology aims to abandon the basic institutions—economic, political those characterize Western society. The term deep ecology enjoys wide currency and considerable charisma in the international environment movement. The term was introduced by Arne Naess, a Norwegian philosophy professor. Deep ecology is a powerful ecology movement. Naess sketched the outlines of an ecological world view. According to the first principle, the identity of each individual, at whatever ontological level, is not rationally autonomous of the rest of the reality. The identity of each individual is determined by its relation with other individuals. All forms of life are equally permitted to live and blossom. Human beings are not ethically privileged. Other life forms are just as morally great as we are. The principles of diversity and symbiosis enhance the opportunities for all beings to live and blossom. The fight against pollution and resource depletion is the part of the ecology movement.

Naess said that we must widen our circle of identification. We identify not merely with our family, our community, our culture, or with humanity as a whole, but also with our immediate environment, the place where we are born or to which we belong, our land, our earth. Naess envisages self-realization as the transition not only from ego to social self, but from social self to ecological self.

When we identify ourselves with nature, our innate self-love expands in proportion to our new sense of self. Our self-interest becomes convergent with the interests of the rest of life. Defence of nature becomes a matter of self-defence. Naess pointed out that the process of self-realisation has affinities with Gandhi's notion of enlightenment. An enlightened being is not alienated from anything. Self-realisation represents the actualization of our greatest potentiality for being. Self-realisation makes our life happy and meaningful. Dave Foreman expressed powerful emotions for the preservation of wilderness and biological diversity in *Confessions of an Eco-Warrior*. Foreman became one of the founders of Earth First!, a more or less apolitical action group. The organization was established in 1980. It employed direct intervention to stop environmentally destructive development, deforestation, and dam building as well as road construction in wilderness areas. Foreman put the role of human beings on the planet:

> Human beings are merely one of the millions of species that have been shaped by the process of evolution for three and a half billion years. According to this view, all living beings have the same right to be here.... A Grizzly Bear snuffling along Pelican Creek in Yellow stone National park with her two cubs has just as much right to life as any human has, and is far more important ecologically. All things have intrinsic value, inherent worth. Their value is not determined by what they will ring on the cash register of the gross national product, or whether or not they are good. They are good because they exist.[3] (3-4)

The organization, Earth First has attracted considerable media attention. It also influenced pro-environmental legislative and judicial decisions. It is a positive force. Foreman said, "We do not engage in radical action, because we are antinomians, but because we are for something—the beauty, wisdom, and abundance of this living planet" (214). Biocentrism is a position full of self-contradictions and absurdities. All life feeds on other life. The only complete biocentrist would be a dead one, who returned his elements to the earth for recycling.

Capitalist industrialist western society desires more and more economic output. Ever increasing need is destroying the planet and subverting the precise mix of elements of required for life to continue. Bookchin is at his best in *Remaking Society: Pathways to a Green Future*. The increase of hierarchy, domination, and exploitation of each other is part and parcel of our domination of nature.

According to Bookchin ecological problems are only one aspect of a system of social domination. Domination extends from human being/nature relationship to the person/person relationship. In the system of domination, both people and nature are degraded into the role of resources for exploitation. Ecology is a social science. It finds hierarchical power relations are at the heart of all forms of exploitation and oppression. Industrial capitalism has commoditized and mechanized the world. According to Bookchin ecological society of the future would replace capitalism with a non-hierarchical model of development. The ecological society would eventually eliminate the use of non-renewable fossil fuels.

Bookchin's *Remaking Society* has the aura of a classic. It is an essential text of social philosophy. Foreman and Bookchin have firmly expressed the view capitalism is unable and futile to solve the ecological problems until they become horrible. Reconstruction of the nature is essential for the progress and sustainable development of human beings.

Foreman was disinclined to the politics of both the left and the right. He believed that economic and social problems are less important than ecological ones. Evils perpetuated by capitalist expansion can be eradicated by environmental vision only. *The Ecology of Freedom* is a dense work on nature.

Murray Bookchin is brilliant, realistic philosopher and utopian idealist. He is at his best in *Remaking Society:*

Pathways to a Green Future. The utopist focuses on the past and the future, the realist on the present. Hunter gatherers lived harmoniously without domination and hierarchy. It was free from the menace of supremacy and patriarchy.

> It is hard for the modern mind to appreciate that precapitalist societies identified social excellence with cooperation rather than competition; disaccumulation rather than accumulation; public service rather than private interest; the giving of gifts rather than the sale of commodities; and care and mutual aid rather than profit and rivalry.[4] (46-47)

The primeval egalitarian society fell through stages. The increase of hierarchy, domination and exploitation of each other is part and parcel of our domination of nature. Hierarchy is responsible for ecological devastation. We should stop devaluation of human. We should preserve social institutions which consider human worth and dignity.

Ecology is a social science. Bookchin expressed the view that ecological problems are one of the aspects of a system based on domination. In such systems people and nature are degraded into the role of resources for exploitation by those on top. According to Fromm hierarchical power relations are the basic reasons of all forms of exploitation and oppression.

Bookchin is one of the most powerful critics of contemporary society. He sees through the hypocrisy, self-deception, and destruction involved in capitalism, Marxism, and certain forms of ecology. Capitalism is ruthless in expansionist policies. It requires more forests, minerals, animals, and people to produce more products. Many of them may be unnecessary but capitalists' main concern is to keep the economy in constant growth. Exploitative and misleading corporations degrade consumers and workers.

Bookchin believed strongly that ecological society of the future will replace capitalism with the non-hierarchical organizations at the local governments. These local political organizations will be direct representation of the population. These communities would take care of local ecosystems. They would abandon the capitalist mentality of "grow or die."

They would wipe out the domination over people and nature by the top levels of a power structure caught in a mentality of domination.

Bookchin's *Remaking Society* has the impression of a classic. It can be treated as an essential text of social philosophy. *Defending the Earth* makes us aware of Foreman's and Bookchin's ideologies. Both Foreman and Bookchin have rightly pointed out capitalism's failure to deal with ecological problems until they become horrible. We should reconstruct nature to ensure future of our children.

Chapter seven is about Aldo Leopold. Fromm emphasizes in Aldo Leopold: Esthetic "Anthropocentrist" that no environmentalist sought literal equality for the subject of his or her concern. Leopold introduced the idea that the use of the earth solely as an economic resource will eventually destroy both it and us. Therefore, ethics must include "soils, waters, plants and animals". Humans should not consider themselves as the sole master of the earth, but plain member and citizen of it. Leopold rightly said:

> A thing is right when it tends to preserve the integrity, stability, and beauty of the biotic community. It is wrong when it tends otherwise.[5]

A land ethic reflects that every individual is responsible for the health of the land. Health is the capacity of the land for self-renewal. He criticizes universal ecological shortsightedness. He has expressed concern for the future of human life and a type of intellectualist arrogance.

The notion of 'wholeness' or 'integrity' has come in for a good deal of post-structuralist criticism. Colours, textures and relationships are mind-dependent. Old 'New Criticism' touchstone of organic unity should be applied in the larger context. Leopold disdains the capitalism's cash nexus. He also acknowledged its inevitability and its attractive side as well.

Aldo Leopold wrote *A Sand Country Almanac*. It was posthumously published in 1949. This book has now achieved scriptural status. Leopold expressed with confidence that the use of the earth solely as an economic resource will eventually destroy both it and us. Human beings behave in a responsible manner as the members of the biotic community and not the conqueror of it. Roderick Nash in *The Rights of Nature* said that "no environmentalist seeks literal equality for the subjects of his or her concern."

A Sand Country Almanac aims to protect an utilizable and beautiful world. Leopold appears at times to safeguard ecosystems at the cost of individual members. Destruction of the forests in the long run is harmful to various human interests, the aesthetic as well as the ecological. Leopold is motivated by aesthetic concerns, rather than concerns about human welfare. Fromm points out that aesthetic response is the most powerful anthropocentric interest of all. It is produced by the very nature and operation of our bodies and psyches.

"Postmodern Ecologizing: Circumference without a Centre" is the chapter eight in the book. In this chapter, Fromm provided the account of Buell's *The Ecological Imagination: Thoreau, Nature Writing, and the Formation of American Culture*. Buell has given the broad account of environmental perception, the place of nature in the history of western thought. He emphasized Thoreau and nature writing in nineteenth century America. He is acquainted with world literature, the other arts, philosophy, history, and criticism. He has remarkable depth of American literary knowledge. He is acquainted with contemporary culture. Buell's writing is the product of his overwhelming vision, strong moral convictions. Buell emphasized that responsiveness to nature is a great cultural value.

In "Postmodern Ecologising: Circumference without a Center", Fromm presents an ecocentric way of life. He related green writing with green thinking and green reading. Buell proposed that literary works have the power to connect environment and everyday life. He laments recent literary theories dissociation of the text, the author and the world. He said emphatically that literature must not take readers always away from the physical world but back to it.

American writing prominently deals with the issues of race, class, and gender. Nature was given a secondary place. One should free oneself from such biases. American pastoralism regards earth as nurturing mother. Earth became the victim of technological meanness. Abbey, Leslie Marmon Silko, and Annie Dillard, and their precursors like Mary Austin made a proposition that pastoral vision can transform a mode of dominion and exploitation to one of green accessibility and ecocentrism. Buell sees a movement from anthropocentrism toward biocentrism. He writes more gracefully.

Buell laments abstract quality of popular environmentalism and its disengagement from everyday life. He proposed that literary works have the power to make the connection of environment and everyday life avidly. He laments recent literary theory's dissociation of the text, the author, and the world. He believed that author as the creator of the text should be given appropriate importance in the analysis of the text. He asked the right question: "*Must literature always lead us away from the physical world, never back to it?*"

He examined American writing related with the issues of race, gender, and class. Buell stated that while arriving at ecocentric state of thinking one should not fall into other biases like environmental racism. Earth is the nurturing mother. It has become a victim of technological callousness. We should see the earth from the perspective of egocentrism, not from a method of domination and exploitation. Buell feels that literary theory should bring association between text and world, rather than dissociation. It is antienvironmental to regard text and world as separate entities having no relation.

Thoreau was sensitive to nature for its own sake. He organized his observations into aesthetic patterns. Thoreau revealed Pastoralism, spiritualism, and sustainable agriculture. He is a motive force in the green ecology.

Chapter nine is entitled as "The "Environment" Is Us." Books dealing with natural science and environment are now a vast industry. A startling number of disciplines have evolved since Leopold's landmark A Sand Country Almanac of 1949. Environmental medicine, environmental history, environmental engineering, environmental ethics, social ecology, green travel, green farming, conservation biology, eco-feminism, ecocriticism, etc. have made their strong presence in the academic circles. Environment literally was the matter that surrounds us. We now understand environment as part of our being, and we being part of it. Individual things are an illusion. Environment is the very essence of human existence in the world.

Bodies in Protest: Environmental Illness and the Struggle over Medical Knoweldge by Steve Kroll-Smith and H. Hugh Floyd is a famous book about environmental illness. Cases of environmental illness are increasing.

Thinking Ecologically: The Next Generation of Environmental Policy is edited by Marian Chertov and Daniel Esty. The book is about the issues of politics, industry, lifestyles, employment, and international relations. More integrated policies can solve environmental problems. The book gives the message of interconnectedness and cooperation. A great deal of information is given about industrial ecology, ecosystem management, property rights, land use, technology, ecological la, automobiles, energy prices, and the global economy.

Fromm in "The "Environment" Is Us" deals with the impact of environment on the health of individuals. Environment is the stuff that surrounds us. Environmental illness is a new way of knowing the body in relationship to built environment. Material world flooded with commodities promises to make life easier and healthier but does the opposite for many people. Environmental illness makes people miserable even though economically they are sound.

The contemporary problem of belief is itself the problem of the unbelievability of truths. Environment is an essential ingredient of production. People are increasingly becoming aware that "the environment" after all is really us. We are not distinct from the environment.

Peter C. van Wyck wrote inclusive and intellectually sophisticated book, *Primitives in the Wilderness: Deep Ecology and the Missing Human Subject*. It is philosophic and self-reflexive. Human beings are just one of the biological elements in the ecosystem. Deep ecologists give importance to intrinsic value of everything, rather than the instrumental value. Trees cannot defend their own intrinsic value. In a Foucauldian ethos all communication is a power strategy. The deep ecologist fails to notice that he is an anthropocentric as anybody else. Every system of thought is a human production determined by societal and personal contingencies. No species is ecocentric, because continued existence depends on looking out for one's own protection.

We live in a multicultural world. The ecological situation differs considerably from country to country. The persons belonging to different cultures have varying attitudes to the environment. Environment is the essence of the real human. People have become aware that environment is not something outside there, but the environment is part of our personality, and we are part of it.

"Ecology and Ecstasy on Interstate 80" is the title of chapter ten. Harold Fromm gives the first-person narration of his experience of pollution. He experienced headaches and malaise in Fullerton, near Disneyland. One of his friends fell into drowsy states several times a day. He observed in West everywhere miles and miles of poisonous air. Toxic air is the fruit of expansionism and technology. It makes millions of people feel wretched every day. It contributes to long-term often fatal diseases. Electric power plants, oil refineries, steel mills, millions of automobiles, dry-cleaning plants, sports-utility vehicles, copper smelters have contributed to the pollution in cities. According to Fromm, technology has become one of the critical problems of contemporary society.

In "Ecology and Ecstasy on Interstate 80", Fromm presents his obsession with ecology. Fromm observes that toxic air has been making millions of people miserable. He emphasises that these are the fruits of expansionism and technology. Fromm said: "To suppose technology is not among contemporary society's chief critical problems would be to live in a fool's paradise, to be permanently out to lunch." The good and bad of human life were mostly technology. Without technology human beings would never have been able to lift themselves out of primal animal existence. The bad and good were inextricably tied together. To be against technology seems to be against human life. Leopold rightly said that biocentrism enhances human life both practical and aesthetic.

The physical relationship between the natural world and individuals is unquestionable. The psychosocial effect of the natural world on the human life is often less concrete. There is the close connection between the environment in which we live and our creativity but it is abstract. Our consciousness is bounded and delimited by our materiality. Our idea of self and our belief in free will derive largely from the physical surrounding.

Ecocritic Harold Fromm has explored the challenging exploration of the relationship of humanity with the natural surroundings. He has expressed his own physical experiences and observations with insights gathered from both the humanities and the sciences. Writing broadly and personally, Fromm explores our views of nature and how we write about it. He ties together ecology, evolutionary psychology, and consciousness studies to show that our perceived separation from our surroundings is an illusory construct. He argues for a naturalistic vision of creativity, free will, and the literary arts unobstructed by common academic and professional chains. At each point of this exploration, Fromm is honest, engaging, and generous.

Fromm's Philosophical, critical, often personal, sweeping interdisciplinary and sometimes argumentative essays will change the way you think about your place in the environment. An individual cannot exist alone. Each individual exists within an environmental field with which he must engage in order to live. He must engage with the objects of his world in order to survive physically; he must have food, clothing, and shelter, or the resources for providing them. He must engage with persons in his environment in order to survive psychologically. Man, then, is both an autonomous individual person and an environmentally oriented person who needs other persons, other social institutions. Both the individual and the environment must be affirmed, studied, and described; and the interaction between them must be affirmed, studied, and described. Man or woman are both an individual, unique phenomenon and also are participants in the social roles imposed by the culture.

The field of Ecocriticism has experienced dramatic growth and dramatic changes since its formal inception in the 1990s Washington. Ecocriticism has attracted scholarly attention, praise, and criticism as the words "environmental crisis" are heard more often in more places. The twenty-first century is a time of excitement and challenge for Ecocriticism.

Although the early 1990s are seen as the formative years of the field, the idea of Ecocriticism had already been explored by scholars in various articles. But it was the publication of Lawrence Buell's *The Environmental Imagination* in 1995 and Cheryll Glotfelty and Harold Fromm's collection, *The Ecocriticism Reader*, in 1996 that solidified Ecocriticism and gave scholars a foundation. The field of Ecocriticism focuses on literature and the environment.

Therefore, combating environmental destruction is directly linked to the fight for personal, social, political, and economic agency. This is another reason for not only recognizing people as part of landscapes, but also analyzing how this affects different communities and cultures.

Technology has made our life easy and happy. Donna Haraway may be right: we're already cyborgs, half organism, half prostheses, half nature, half technology. Biotechnological medicine protects us from many fatal diseases. Good and bad are inextricably tied together. To oppose technology completely is wrong. We should be the master of technology, but not the slaves of technology.

The major motive for human beings is human endurance and its attendant happiness. Aldo Leopold made a significant contribution to biocentrism. People realized suicidal human devastation is the result of narrow vision and ignorance. Leopold offered biocentrism to enhance human life aesthetically and practically.

Human life is strongly based on the ecosystem. War and unbridled capitalist/communist technologies have endangered planet, earth. Protecting nature is in our best interests. David Ehrenfeld wrote about the failures of modern technology in *The Arrogance of Humanism*. Our study of nature is study of ourselves as we are inseparable part of nature. Nature provides us with profound vision and ecstasy for life. "Full Stomach Wilderness and the Suburban Esthetic" is the title of chapter eleven. Fromm joined the environmental movement in the early seventies. He experienced nightmare, physical and psychological illness resulted from pollution. He became an ecologically committed writer. He started campaigns against pollution.

Fromm made the proposition that wilderness is a modern invention. It is an aesthetic object, a rhetorical device. Astonishing beauty of the mountain inspires people. Suburban developments have created much of the beautiful areas in Tucson and other places. Wilderness becomes an object of contemplation, when development spreads to the place.

Development technology is creative and destructive force. An open-ended negotiation between technology's good and evil effects will resolve the issue of cohabitation with nature and technology. Creation or destruction is based on values springing from ever altering human subjectivities. When enough damage has been done, people realize importance of environment and they start the work of reconstruction. Because of narrow perspective people neglect environment. Fromm has emphasized the truth that human life requires limitations to survive urban and suburban development. When we become aesthetic we know the value of limitations. When we are assured of full stomach, we realize the aesthetics of nature.

"Coetzee's Postmodern Animals" is chapter twelve in the book. Coetzee is a postmodern author. He is particularly sympathetic to women. In *In the Heart of the Country*, he expressed the concerns of women in the effective manner. In the contemporary world foundations of belief are radically damaged. There is the urgent need to reconstruction of it. He values the sense of being. He revealed his ideas of sense of being in his 1983 Booker Prize novel, *Life and Times of Michael K*. The protagonist of the novel wanders around South Africa during an imagined time of what amounts to civil war between minority whites and majority blacks. He does not care about what is happening. As a conscious being certain things impinge on his consciousness. He is mainly concerned to survive in personal freedom. He neither takes the side of blacks nor whites. Coetzee has presented the issue of personal existentialism skillfully. He has revealed the sense of concrete being during a time of the collapse of traditional South African society at the end of Apartheid.

Peter Singer wrote a landmark book, *Animal Liberation*. It was first published in 1975. J.M. Coetzee presented an ethical problem philosophically in *The Lives of Animals*. There are short stories about fiction writer, Elizabeth Costello. Costello informs her audience the horrors animals suffer through human abuse. It is primarily concerned with the pain and suffering we impose on animals. He recommended vegetarian diet.

Coetzee commented on new social order in his novel, *Disgrace*. New social order is not charming. Social order based on ethical values is charming. A Skeptical wise man sees too much for his own good.

Part two of book is related with Nature and Evolution. "My Science Wars" is the title of chapter thirteen. Paul R. Gross and Norman Levitt published *Higher Superstition: The Academic Left and Its Quarrels with Science* in 1994. Ross identified the collapse of western civilization. Cultural Studies has emphasized the need of reconstruction of the western civilization. Levitt and Gross are liberal in their perspectives. They defended the basic reasonableness of science. They are scientists who speak the issues and languages of the humanities with exemplary sophistication as men of wide-ranging culture. Their writing is clear, insightful, and witty. They also acknowledged the errors and evils that flow from science's involvement with uncontrolled capitalist technology. Levitt and Gross object to the notion that feminist science uses a different reason from male science.

Paglia Camille wrote the book *Vamps and Tramps*. She is an accomplished synthesizing public intellectual. Her work speaks for itself. She says what she feels and believes.

In 1990, Paglia published *Sexual Personae*. Her writing is vital and adroit. Her outlook is perfectly clear in *Sexual Personae*:

> Society is an artificial construction, a defence against nature's power…civilized man conceals from himself the extent of his subordination to nature…. Sexuality and eroticism are the intricate intersection of nature and culture. Feminists grossly oversimplify the problem of sex when they reduce it to a matter of social convention: readjust society, eliminate sexual inequality, purify sex roles and happiness and harmony will reign…. For Sade, getting back to nature…would be to give free rein to violence and lust. I agree. Society is not the criminal but the force which keeps crime in check…. Sex is power. Identity is power. In western culture, there are no unexploitative relationships.[6] (*SP*, 1-2)

The knowledge provided in the book is as fresh as ever because of Paglia's unflagging vivacity. She attacks truism among feminists and Focauldians that human beings are socially constructed. She reaffirms that nature runs the show. We should not fail to acknowledge nature's power over us. It leads to an arrogance of social institutions. We should respect society as our strongest defence. We should not forget the truth that nature sustains the society. She emphasized nature and nurture in culture. She conserves values in cultures. She catches the air and aroma of contemporary life in her speech and writing. She defends literature against politics. She richly deserves the fame. She is a person of integrity. Nature is God for her. Corrosive capitalism impacted daily life of the people. Democracy's freedom threatens to undermine democracy itself.

Chapter fifteen, "A Crucifix for Dracula: Wendell Berry Meets Edward O. Wilson" reflects the synthesis of all the knowledge disciplines. Edward Wilson is one of those daunting scientists who write extremely well. He knows several fields deeply. His book on sociobiology is a founding text in the field of evolutionary biology. He promotes a new synthetical direction for all knowledge disciplines. He remarks:

> The assumptions they made of a lawful material world, the intrinsic unity of knowledge, and the potential of indefinite human progress are the ones we still take most readily into our hearts, suffer without, and find maximally rewarding through intellectual advance. The greatest enterprise of the mind has always been and always will be the attempted linkage of the sciences and humanities. The ongoing fragmentation of knowledge and resulting chaos in philosophy are not reflections of the real world but artifacts of scholarship. The propositions of original Enlightenment are increasingly favored by objective evidence, especially from the natural sciences.[7]

Wilson is conservative in thinking. He believes in truth, a real world, human mind power, and the pre-eminence of the sciences. For him, the astonishing feats of the mind are not finally the result of the metaphysical intuition, faith, grace, or Platonic reminiscence but, rather are the achievements of the human brain.

The fragmentation of the knowledge opposes any sort of coherent management of the problems of the mankind. The divide between the sciences and the humanities prevents a clear view of the world as it really is.

Human faculties are not creations from above. They are the outcome of the human interaction with nature. They are based on material processes. Species can survive in congenial environments. Sociobiology regards social customs and behaviours as offshoots of our biological needs. According to Wilson, natural selection is being more and more influenced by social, psychological, and intellectual developments. Natural selection is the part of a reciprocal relationship.

Edward Wilson explains in his ecological manifesto, *The Diversity of Life*, human beings need rainforests, earth's microorganisms, and the variety of creatures in order to survive on this particular planet, Earth. Human nature took millions of years to develop. Ecology has made us the species we are.

Religion possesses strength to the extent that it codifies and puts into permanent form the highest values of humanity consistent with the empirical knowledge. Wilson concludes his book with the expression of the need of humankind to come to terms with the earth. His central claim is that we have been produced out of the materials of the earth and can never cut ourselves loose from our earthly underpinnings, no matter how sublime our thoughts.

Wendell Berry, a Kentucky farmer, is a prolific poet who has written poems, fiction, and essays on ecological themes. He loathes present global economy for its downright disregard of cultural and natural foundation of human life. He is an eminent cultural guide through his creative works, *The Unsettling of America* and *A Continuous Harmony*. Berry has done excellent writing in and for wilderness.

Our perspectives are shaped by our needs. Ancient nomadic desert population's perspectives were shaped by their own needs. Berry righty complaints that applied science allied itself with corporate capitalism. Farming and farmers are being destroyed by the global economy. Faceless and exploitative corporations have taken over farmers and farmlands. Contemporary corporate forces have been destroying institutions, customs and habitats of one's formative years. Wilson criticizes academic professions for their narrow-mindedness, self-interest, and radical ignorance of the ecological roots of all earthly existence.

Chapter sixteen, "The New Darwinism in the Humanities" describes human civilisation and culture. Mammals did not emerge until about two hundred million years ago. Reasonably familiar looking animals entered the scene only a mere sixty-five million years ago, after the end of the dinosaurs. *Homo sapiens* took over fifty to a hundred thousand years ago. Hunter-gatherer phase of hominids lasted for millions of years until only ten thousand years ago. The advent of farming introduced the settled communities we regard as civilisation, which transformed human life in every conceivable way, setting off a rapid and conscious development of the arts and sciences.

Hominid brain took billions of years to evolve. Human mind cannot be separate from its material origins. It is not a magical self-sustaining faculty. Our very material limitations enable us to be the creatures we are.

Steven Pinker affords a rich account of the foundations of Darwinian interventions in *The Blank Slate: The Modern Denial of Human Nature*. Emile Durkheim expressed a sentiment whose influence shaped the social sciences for almost a century:

> Collective representations, emotions, and tendencies are caused not by certain states of the consciousness of individuals but by the conditions in which the social group, in its totality, is placed. Such actions can, of course materialize only if the individual natures are not resistant to them; but these individual natures are merely the indeterminate material that the social factor molds and transforms.[8] (Cosmodes and Tooby)

Pinker gives a fatal blow to the dying orthodox notion of the blank slate. Pinker and E.O. Wilson are science thinkers. They have mastered the basics of contemporary human culture. The matter of "beauty" in the arts is a complex term.

Carrol's magnum opus, *Evolution and Literary Theory* is a powerful attack against post-structuralism and textualism and their leading exponents, Derrida, Foucault, and their many disciples. Textualism is the belief that knowledge of the world is only knowledge of the text only. In such a universe of discourse, one opinion is as good as another. Everything becomes indeterminate.

Carrol expressed the view that, "the subject matter of literature is human experience." Product of culture and rhetoric have influenced human world. Human world is made of ground up. Fiction deals with the personal interactions constituted primarily by combinations of motives. Poststructuralism had kept aside the material foundations of human life. Human nature is derived from the material base. Carrol interconnects literature with evolution and ecology. He explicates in "The Ecology of Victorian Fiction" the relation between the organism and the environment in which the animal is living:

> No organism can be understood except in it interactive relations with its total environment. An organism is never an isolated thing. By definition and in brute reality the world that an organism inhabits is part of the organism. The organism carries that world embedded and moulded [sic] into every inmost fold of its physiology, its anatomy, and its psyche.... The felt quality of experience within a natural world is one of those fundamental conditions of experience. It should also be one of the fundamental categories of literary analysis.[9] (302)

Darwinian adaptationism and ecology has produced the discipline of behavioural ecology. The insights of behavioural ecology have great power on the creation and interpretation of literary works. The Darwinians believe that the core of our being is given. Human nature is expressible in innumerable ways.

Culture has a great force. It influences the growth and development of the human beings largely. All life forms are dependent on nature for their survival. We must reconnect ourselves to nature.

Chapter seventeen "Ecocriticism's Big Bang" is about the origin and development of the literary theory-ecocriticism. The genre of ecocriticism appeared in the 1990s. For centuries from Virgil's Georgic to John Clare, Thoreau, Rachel Carson, sensitive people had actually realized that their life is placed in the nature.

A new professional organization, the Association for the Study of Literature and Environment has been formed in 1991. A new journal, *Interdisciplinary Studies in Literature and Environment* has been launched. A new canonical text, *The Ecocriticism Reader: Landmarks in Literary Ecology* is produced by Cheryll Glotfelty and Harold Fromm.

Ecocriticism brought together writers who write about nature. Ecocriticism includes ecology of cities, environmental racism, environmental law, capitalism and colonial exploitation. Ecocriticism acknowledges the explanatory power of evolutionary biology and evolutionary psychology.

Human beings live in an environment. They are semi-independent of the environment in which they live. They are harming environment with pollution, toxics, erosion, and water usage. The environment makes the person. Fromm describes clearly human life in the context of nature:

> A man and a woman eat food from the earth that becomes their bodies and sperm cells and eggs. A fertilized egg, fed by more plants and animals, keeps dividing, turning into specialized body parts, including a brain, that are wholly derived from the plants and animals and the earth, sunlight, water, air, etc., that generate them. (*The Nature of Being Human*, p. 190)

The fetus becomes a baby who becomes a person. The substance of a person is generated from the earth. The person is the environment and the environment is the person. Human beings work hard to get their livelihood. Human brain is a fantastically complex machine made of hundreds of billions of neurons that produce the sense of consciousness, sight, smell, touch, hearing, and self. Neuroscientists tell us that environment produces the desires, actions and attitudes among the human beings.

We are subject to the environment. Nature influences physical and psychological condition of the people. The period in which there was nothing outside the text has passed. Real world begins to seem very real indeed.

Glen A. Love introduces ecocriticism effectively in *Practical Ecocriticism: Literature, Biology and the Environment*. He provides enormously wide and deep knowledge of ecocriticism and Darwinian sciences. He describes the connection of humanity to the planet. He suggests the implications of biology both for literature and life. He has given new meaning to diversity. He interweaves the connections between nature and humanity. He has provided extensive reflections on Leo Marx, Raymond Williams, Virgil and Theocritus, Lawrence Buell, Joseph Meeker, C.P. Snow and others. *Practical Ecocriticism* is an ideal book; Love has been highly persuasive and skilled in establishing close relationship between humanity and nature.

Chapter eighteen in the book is entitled as "Overcoming the Oversoul: Emerson's Evolutionary Existentialism." Emerson expressed a profound sense of nature, challenge and promise of mental emancipation. His first book *Nature* was published in 1838. Morality had been the major theme of the book. German idealism and romantic subjectivism influenced him greatly. He asked to reconcile the materialism and spiritual values. He perceived human beings as completely woven into the material web of life. He saw human life as moral despite its radical materiality.

In recent years the distinction between nature and nurture has been gradually eroded. Matt Ridley's *Nature via Nurture,* Daniel Dennett's *Freedom Evolves*, William Calvin's *A Brain for All Seasons*, Pinker, and E.O. Wilson gradually arrive at the conclusion that genes switch on and off depending on environment, and physical and mental states of the mind. Peter Singer and Roderick Nash have expressed the importance of the widening circle of human empathy. Nature and culture develop human nature.

Chapter nineteen entitled, "Back to Bacteria": Richard Dawkins' Fabulous Bestiary is a reverse journey from *Homo sapiens* to the primal blob. It is a magnum opus. Dawkins gives us an account of the evolution of human life on the plane of earth. Human and all other life forms have emerged from the blobs of bacteria. Richard Dawkins' *The Ancestors Tale* is a dazzling, four billion year pilgrimage to the origins of life. It is an account of the reverse journey from present day humans back to the microbial beginnings of life. It is a journey happily narrated by meetings of fellow modern animals, as well as plants, fungi, and bacteria. The text gives astonishing information about the intimate relationship of human life with the rest of the world. In the evolutionary sequence fungus appears first, then the rest of the multicellular organisms, then plants, and finally single celled microbes, the very foundational elements in the origins of life.

The Ancestor's Tale is a reverse journey of sorts from *Homo sapiens* to the primal blob. It is a retro history of evolution back to the parent of us all. The life evolved out of nearly nothing, some 10 billion years after the universe evolved out of nothing. Living things are collections of molecules like other things in nature. The real world narrated in *The Ancestor's Tale* is fantastic.

The part three of the book is about the concept of consciousness. Chapter twenty is given the title, "Muses, Spooks, Neurons and the Rhetoric of Freedom." Creativity seems magical, implausible, and involuntary. The chapter twenty deals about the issues of the stream of consciousness. Experts report that there are at least 50 billion neurons. One fifty billion may be storing the data of our lives. Without motivations there would not be nay behaviour at all. Neurons are "brain cells" which establish body-mind interaction. The billions of brain cells interact by means of their thread like dendrites and axons to produce one million billion connections known as synapses. An electrochemical transmission takes place across these synapses triggered by stimulation from anywhere in the body and from different areas of the brain. Daniel M. Wegner in *The Illusion of Conscious Will* tells a great deal about conscious.

> The fact is, each of us acts in response to an unwieldy assortment of mental events, only a few of which may be easily brought to mind and understood as conscious intentions that cause our.[10] (Wegner, 145)

The nature of neuronal storage is an unsolved mystery. Brain is not the storehouse of representational materials. The neuronal storage of the brain is like a digital compact disc. Codes exist in the consciousness to produce scene. Neuroscientists opine that consciousness is produced ad hoc over and over again each microsecond by some of the million billion synapses.

Wegner tells about the action and memory: "Actions and their meanings are stored separately in memory. Otherwise, we would always know exactly what we intend and never suffer the embarrassment of walking into a room and wondering what it was we wanted there" (Wegner, 166).

Writer like everyone else is socially constructed. The author is constructed by billions of involuntary neurons with a vast prehistory, constantly reformulated by culture. The time and place one lives, one's parents, one's education, one's temperament, bodily states and infirmities, desires, tastes, traumas, joys form one's life. One's ability to follow instruction depends on the contents and dispositions of one's mental storage facility. Creative writer is a passive agent of neuronal storage, energy and organization. Virtual self cannot create anything.

People are trapped in constant paradigms not by their choice but compulsion. The self cannot initiate a thing because self is an effect. Self is like a character on the movie screen. We are changing all the time, growing, learning. Self does not generate the change. Something cannot exist out of chain of causes. We change and influence behaviour of other people. People are changed unwittingly. People are changed by rhetoric, muses or spooks, narrative generating neurons. People are unpredictable, despite all their character defining predictability. Because we can never know the ultimate springs of their behaviour. Biochemistry is imprinted in a preconscious way. Human behaviour is a form of rhetorical music. We are pretty brilliant robots.

Chapter twenty-one "John Searle and His Ghosts" deals with human consciousness. Cognitive neuroscientists such as Gerald Edelman and Walter Freeman have given highly technical maps of the brain showing neurons, electrochemical forces, inputs and outputs, recursive transmission paths. Descartes tried and failed to bridge the mind/body divide. John Searle writes strikingly lucid prose. He deals with the three main problems of contemporary philosophy of mind: consciousness, free will, and the self. He has given final blow to the age old positions of dualism and materialism that he regards as obsolete.

According to Searle consciousness is produced from the same materials as everything else—physical micro particles of various types. He identified its unique characteristics. Understanding is one of the important functions of the consciousness. Behaviour of the neurons forms the consciousness. Subjective first person can experience subjective consciousness. Action of neurons determines the total state, mental state of an individual.

Searle has taken a worthwhile survey of historical positions. He is aware of developments in the neurosciences. He has given an elaborate account of human consciousness.

Chapter twenty-two is entitled, "Daniel Dennett and the Brick Wall of Consciousness." Daniel Dennett has written classic books on human consciousness, *Consciousness Explained* (1991) and *Darwin's Dangerous Idea* (1995). The books deal with the matters of self, consciousness and free will. The human brain involves nearly 100 billion neurons. These are a variety of fine, threadlike long brain cells. They link to brain internal organs of the body. Within the brain these neurons connect with each other via synapses across which neural impulses send electrochemical messages. Harold Fromm said that the sheer number of connections is greater than the number of stars in the universe. The network is the place where the performance of the body is registered. All forms of psychological experience takes place, cerebration, emotion arise in this network of neurons.

There is no stable existing behind all the neuronal flux of your brain. There is not coherent narrative in the human consciousness. Signals vie like sperm cells to get to consciousness. Winners get entry into the line of the stream of consciousness. Without a centre the self is virtual. Life is produced from nonlife. Our consciousness is produced from multitudes of unconscious firings. Pandemonium of neuronal activity generates our behaviour and thoughts. Consciousness is ultimately composed of material particles that are electrochemical firings.

David Chalmers, author of *The Conscious Mind: In Search of a Fundamental Theory* opposed the view that consciousness is not something over and above electrochemical firings. He does not believe that materialism can answer the question of consciousness. According to him the problem of consciousness is the problem of experience. When we think and perceive, there is a whir of information-processing. Experience depends on the physical features of the world.

According to Chalmers, there is something about consciousness over and above data processing. Consciousness is not a mystery. It is a physical, biological phenomenon. Chalmers explains consciousness: "It seems to many people that consciousness is a mystery, the most wonderful magic show imaginable, an unending series of specific effects that defy explanation. I think that they are mistaken: consciousness is a physical, biological phenomenon-like metabolism or reproduction" (Sweet Dreams, 57). Chalmers' magnum opus of 1996, *The Conscious Mind*, describes consciousness.

Chapter twenty-three, "The Crumbing Mortar of Social Construction" emphasises the elements which construct society. Steven Pinker demolished the quaint notion of the human mind as a blank slate. Any society constructs customs or machinery, motivated by the human biological programme. Culture constructs society. Culture can alter the bodies and psyches up to a point. The alterations are always shaped and limited by the human nature they are addressing. The human nature can change over time through natural selection. Culture is always at the service of the human nature. Ideologies and thinking can only form what is there, not what is not there. Bodies and brains in the society are directed by the nature.

Fromm concludes the book *The Nature of Being Human: From Environmentalism to Consciousness* by explaining the effects of the environment on body and consciousness in, "My Life as a Robot." Toxic substances, pollution, the quality of soil in which food is grown, living near highways, chlordane, PCBs, DDT, global warming, lead in paint and dishes are more than casually related to one's physical and mental condition. The environment of the planet has evolved us. Neuro scientists and cognitive scientists have claimed that a network of billions of synapses are a self-directing system, that produces us as already mapped out but seemingly flexible psychological beings. We are sometimes bemused by the tragic-comic illusion of autonomy. One cannot understand oneself without a perception. There is nothing to consciousness that is not physical. Myriad elements of the environment are woven into physical being of every person. Nature influences our feelings and how do we exist.

There is the distinction between a robot and a human being. Human beings can ponder or reflect. We feel a consciousness within us. The material of reflection can come from what is already stored in neurons of an individual. It cannot come directly from outside. We can engage in spiritual activity.

Every person has a powerful influence on other people. We can refine the influence through our knowledge of human nature, social expressions, sensitivity, intelligence, and awareness with regard to human behaviour. Human nature has been subject to change for millions of years. Institutions protect the civilized life. Criminals should not be forgiven if they endanger the very existence of society through their deceitful activities.

We should join together to create world in which plants or animals can live together harmoniously.

REFERENCES

1. Foreman, Dave. *Confessions of an Eco-Warrior*. New York: Harmony Books, 1999.
2. Bookchin, Murray. *Remaking Society: Pathways to a Green Future*. Boston: South End Press, 1990.
3. Chase, Steve. *Defending the Earth: A Dialogue Between Murray Bookchin and Dave Foreman*. Boston: South End Press, 1991.
4. Bookchin, Murray. *Remaking Society: Pathways to a Green Future*. Boston: South End Press, 1990.
5. Leopold, Aldo. *A Sand Country Almanac*. New York: Oxford University Press, 1987.
6. Paglia, Camille. *Sexual Personae: Art and Decadence from Nefertiti to Emily Dickinson*. New Haven, Connecticut, 1990.
7. Wilson, Edward. *Consilience: The Unity of Knowledge*. New York: Alfred A. Knopf, 1998.
8. Durkheim, Emily. *Moral Education*. New York: Dover Publications, 2011.
9. Carrol, Joseph. *Evolution and the Literary Theory*. Columbia: University of Missouri Press, 1995.
10. Wegner, Daniel. *The Illusion of Conscious Will*. Cambridge MA.: MIT Press, 2002.

4

Lawrence Buell

Lawrence Buell (Born-1939)

Author of The Future of Environmental Criticism

Professor Lawrence Buell earned an A.B. at Princeton University. He enrolled at Cornell University for Ph.D. He was a professor at Oberlin College before moving to Harvard in 1990. He served as the Harvard College Dean of Undergraduate Education from 1992-96. He chaired the Department of English and American Literature and Language. He also served on the graduate committee for degree in the study of American civilization. He taught course in the American Literature and culture. He has a particular interest in the discourse of the environmental studies, issues of cultural nationalism, and postcolonial literature.

He is the author of *Literary Transcendentalism* (1973), *New England Literary Culture* (1986), *The Environmental Imagination: Thoreau, Nature Writing, and the Formation of American Culture* (1995), *Emerson* (2003), *The Future of Environmental Criticism* (2005), and *Writing for an Endangered World: Literature, Culture, and Environment in the United States and Beyond* (2001). He is co-editor, with Wai Chee Dimock, of *Shades of the Planet: American Literature as World Literature* (2007). He is one of the pioneers of ecocriticism.

Lawrence Buell received Jay Hubbell Medal for Life Time Achievement in American Literary studies in 2007. He won Warren-Brooks Award for outstanding literary criticism in 2003 for his book *Emerson*. He has got John G. Cawelti Award for his *Writing for an Endangered World: Literature, Culture, and Environment in the United States and Beyond*. He retired from Harvard in 2011. Buell's has made significant research in Literature in a Globalizing World, Discourses of Literature and Environment, Theory of National Fiction, Transmutations of Genre in Anglophone Writing, Literature and/of Friendship.

Environmental crisis brings a crisis of imagination. In our time there is the need to find new ways to understand nature and humanity's relation to it. Lawrence Buell takes up the challenge of finding new paths of understanding nature and our relation to it in *The Environmental Imagination*. He develops a new vision of environmental writing. He seeks a new way of conceiving the relationship between human imagination and environmental actuality in the age of industrialization. He gives us a far-reaching account of environmental perception. He provides a major new understanding of Thoreau's achievement. He provides a profound rethinking of our literary and cultural reflections on nature.

The field of ecological criticism is immense in its duration and range. Human beings are inescapably biohistorical creatures who construct themselves through engagement with the surrounding nature. We cannot inhabit outside the environment. In principle the critical exploration begins from the oldest surviving literary text like the Sumerian epic, Gilgamesh, to the literary work produces in our time, like Robert Pogue Harrison's *Forests*. Environment is a more pressing and multifarious problem in the twenty-first century than ever before. W.E.B. Du Bois famously remarked, the key problem of the twentieth century was the racial confrontation. According to W.E.B. Du Bois the most pressing problem in the twenty-first century will be the sustainability of Earth's environment.

The Jay B. Hubbell Award is given each year to a scholar who has made an extraordinary contribution to the study of American literature over the course of his or her career. In 2007, committee members recognized Professor Lawrence Buell for his outstanding work. He has both deepened and widened the traditions of American literature. Lawrence Buell has made two such contributions, first to the study of literary transcendentalism, and second to environmental criticism. For over three decades, he has been widely acknowledged as a leading interpreter of transcendentalist aesthetics. More recently, his work on environmental criticism has shaped the establishment of that field, such that no one writing in it can do so without acknowledging his formative influence.

Professor Buell enlarged the impact of his work on literature and the environment with his next book, *Writing for an Endangered World*, which won the 2001 John G. Cawelti Award for the Most Outstanding Scholarly Inquiry into American Culture, sponsored by the Popular Culture Association and the American Culture Association. While *The Environmental Imagination* addresses the green tradition in American writing, *Writing for an Endangered World* extends the work of environmental criticism to the urban landscape in a transnational context. Covering a diverse range of 19th and 20th century English and American writers, from Thomas Hardy to Joy Harjo, this book puts natural and artificial environments in "conversation with each other," as Buell puts it, and puts an end to the stereotypical conception associating environmental criticism with whiteness.

His most recent book, *The Future of Environmental Criticism*, published in 2005, completes his trilogy on criticism and the environment. It also constitutes a critical introduction to the field in which he himself has played such an influential role. This book, written with the same elegance and theoretical acumen that characterize his earlier work, signals the transformation of environmental criticism from an emergent field into an established research area that is global in scope. Not coincidentally, it has been translated into Japanese and is being translated into Chinese.

These translations are a fitting acknowledgment of the book's scope, of the expanding significance of Lawrence Buell's career, and of the turn it has taken most recently with his co-editing of *Shades of the Planet: American Literature as World Literature*, with Wai Chee Dimock. In this collection, ten prominent scholars of American literature join Buell in relocating the field within an international framework, measuring its significance, as Buell puts it in his contribution to the collection, on a planetary scale, where, to quote Maxine Hong Kingston, it "translates well." So too does Lawrence Buell's own work, both as a critic and as an advocate for American literature and the environment. The defining issue of the 21st century may be the problem of ensuring a decent future for life on the planet.

Literature and the Environment

Buell said that the Arts and Humanities have to make decisive contributions toward full understanding of the various environmental challenges facing the world today. He has both deepened and widened the traditions of American literature.

Emerson was an antislavery activist. He possessed a poetic spirit and multifaceted curiosity about religion and about himself from the very childhood. Intellectual vitality is self-sustaining. Nationalism is nature based. Environmental imagination is the barometer of national imagination. Natural and social environments impinge encroach on each other. Art is the prototype of all creative thoughts. Nature writers portray the world through environmental motifs. It is finally not a matter of word making alone. It makes life and world as well. Artists make the world. High literature reinvents the world through words. Physical nature has tremendous potential to energise the powers of the human mind. We should be awakened to the interdependence of human mind and nature. We have to strengthen bond with nature to overcome spiritual and psychic fragmentation.

Nature is a vital force. It perpetually shapes human and non-human beings. It expands vision, insight and power. It is an important force in human affairs. Emerson is a cultural nationalist. He presented the values that stand the test of time and unite the world. He emphasised the scholar's intellectual independence. He said, "Truth is knowable only by independent minded individuals." He was influenced by the foreign models.

Emerson is a great philosopher and social critic. His writings have been included in the body of the world literature. He had a passion for classical Persian poetry. He speaks across the borders of place and time. He was well aware that one can't uproot oneself wholly from one's home context. He is a religious thinker also. He explicated the importance of religion in human life.

Ecocriticism makes most coherent sense. It brings humanities and sciences together. According to Emerson the spirit of freedom is omnipresent and immortal.

Discourses of environment have become crucial today. We have neglected environment for many decades of the twentieth century. Many nations of the world have been facing the consequences of environmental disaster on human life. The Kenyan environmental activist Wangari Maathai was awarded the Nobel Peace Prize in 2004. Modern industrial society has failed to manage unintended environmental consequences. Issues of vision, value, culture and imagination are very helpful to solve contemporary environmental crises. British ecocritic Dominic Head suggested:

> There is an inextricable tie between individual and community. Culture binds individual and community. Thoreau emphasised the relationship between culture and environment. He said very emphatically that culture depends for its health on environmental health. According to Lawrence Buell environmental crisis involves a crisis of the imagination. We need to develop better ways of imaging nature. We have to be more imaginative in humanity's

> relationship with nature. There is the need to set limits to techno-economic growth. "How we image a thing, true or false, affects our conduct toward it, the conduct of nations as well as persons."[1] (*The Environmental Imagination*)

Aesthetics can become a decisive force for or against environmental change. Human history is implicated in natural history. Forster seriously considered the influence of natural environment shapes emotions, behaviour and art. William Wordsworth's "Nutting" suggests human accountability to the environment.

Leo Marx's *The Machine in the Garden* acknowledges that environment influences culture, text, and personality. We ought to consider environment as the major subject of concern. It should not be the mystification of some other human interests. Raymond Williams and Leo Marx are the most seminal theorists of the country-city polarity. Emerson said with strong confidence that country living stimulates the mind better than city life.

Environmental literary criticism offers a way forward. He assessed the future of environmental literary criticism positively. He pointed toward four crucial challenges: organization, professional legitimation, defining unique models of critical investigation and establishing the significance beyond academy.

Buell's book offers a critical engagement with the field of ecocriticism. According to Cheryll Glotfelty, Ecocriticism is the study of the relationship between literature and the physical environment. His books, *The Environmental Imagination* and *Writing for an Endangered World* have become the important texts in Ecocriticism.

Lawrence Buell is one of the leading theorists in Ecocriticism. *The Future of Environmental Criticism* is a critical review of the ecocritical movement. He has made the proposition that the discourses of the environment should become a permanent part of the literary and cultural studies.

Environmental Justice Movement has made a tremendous effect on the Ecocriticism. Ecocritics have expressed the deep commitment for those people who have been marginalized from the natural world and from the benefits of resources. Ecocritics' work primarily focuses on literature.

Love's *Practical Ecocriticism* is an exploration of, "what it means to be human". Ecocriticism is capable of creating its own critique of environmental literature. All texts can be read as environmental texts. The interests of ecocriticism and environmental history are linked. Without biospheric and planetary conditions human life could not exist.

Buell has mentioned four points that characterize an environmentally oriented work: The non-human environment is present not only as a framing device but as a presence that begins to suggest that human history is implicated in natural history. The human interest is not understood to be the only legitimate interest. Human accountability to the environment is part of the text's ethical orientation. Some sense of the environment as a process rather than as a constant or a given is at least implicit in the text.

Leo Marx announced the end of nature in *The Machine in the Garden* (1964). He delineated the increasing domination of machine civilization in America. Rachel Carson's the best selling *Silent Spring* is about the environmental complexity. She argued that it is impossible for human beings to get complete control over nature. Love believed as Carson had, that "The most important function of literature today is to redirect human consciousness to a full consideration of its place in a threatened natural world." This task demands the personal ethical commitment. Ecocriticism challenges much postmodern critical discourse as well as to the critical systems of the past. Ecocriticism offers a broad vision of life and our place in nature.

Buell believes the crisis originates in consciousness. Writers can help to ameliorate it through their writing. Environmentally conscious literature helps us immensely to find "better ways of imaging nature and humanity's relation to it." Buell asks writers and humanistic scholars to participate in rescue operation of the environment. Albert Gore stated that "We must make the rescue of the environment the central organizing principle for civilization."[2]

Buell believed that Thoreau is relevant for the twenty-first century. Thoreau was an original thinker. Buell shows that Emerson played a more important part in the crusade against slavery than many readers today realize.

Barry Lopez in *Landscape and Narrative* explained the relationship between the external landscape and the interior landscape:

> I think of two landscapes—one outside the self, the other within, the external landscape is the one we see—not only the line and color of the land and its shading at different times of the day, but also its plants and animals in season, its weather, its geology, the record of it climate and evolution.... One learns a landscape finally not by knowing the name or identity of everything in it—but by perceiving the relationship in it—like that between the sparrow and the twig....[3]
>
> The second landscape I think of is an interior one, a kind of projection within a person of a part of the exterior landscape...the speculations, intuitions, and formal ideas we refer to as "mind" are a set of relationships in the interior landscape with purpose and order.... The interior landscape responds to the character and subtlety of an exterior landscape, the shape of the individual is affected by land as it is by genes. (*Arctic Dreams*)

Mary Austin has described environment rather than human interest stories in her famous work *The Land of Little Rain* (1903). She is the authoritative voice of the West and of Native American Culture. She has presented a mature environmental vision through her book. Land is the protagonist. She has explained the patterns of life created by the scarcity of water.

There is the need to strengthen environmental proficiency in twenty-first century. Burroughs, Ruskin or Lawrence, have not believed that the poet or essayist should teach ornithology. The potency of the environmental text consisted not just in the reader's transaction with it. It consists in reanimating and redirecting the reader's transaction with nature.

Modern urbanization has brought about a change in the people's relationship with the nature. Environmental knowledge is very important for the survival of the society in the true sense of the term. Our apparent success at regulating the environment has created the impression that human affairs are not in fundamental ways subject to regulation by the environment. The blindness to the environment produces unintended destabilizing consequences like skin lesions from the ozone hole, owing partly to the products of cooling technologies that have insulated us from confronting the disgrace of our environmental dependence. There is the urgent need that all people should be environmentally literate.

Thoreau is the patron saint of American environmental writing. He struggled hard for the deep understanding of nature. Eminence did not come to him easily. He remained obscure for more than a generation after his death. Thoreau spent his entire career for the study of nature and culture. He is the most representative artist of American culture. He represented nature exquisitely. Emerson explicated that the individual's mystical relation to nature is promising. Classic American pastoral writing constitutes the social vision.

Thomas Jefferson had agrarian roots. Jefferson presented agrarian vision of America in *Notes on the State of Virginia*, ironically on the eve of industrial revolution. He presented the ideal farming. According to him, "the ethos of farming empowers, not frustrates, the pursuit of culture" (p. 41). Pastoral comprises political discourse. Thoreau delivered a lecture "Slavery in Massachusetts" (1854). Thoreau declared that the late events in Boston seem to have permanently shaken our peaceful lives:

> Who can be serene in a country where both the rulers and the ruled are without principle? The remembrance of my country spoils my walk. My thoughts are murder to the state, and involuntarily go plotting against her.

F. Scott Fitzgerald dramatized the conflict between the ideal nature and the emergent technocracy sponsored by the Middle America. Nature is one of the pre-eminently formative influences in traditional if not in contemporary American writing. Influence of nature is seen as a positive cultural value.

Aldo Leopold's *A Sand County Almanac* (1949) clusters a series of essays, prose poems and anecdotes. He aimed to create a symbiosis of art and polemic. Ecological environmental representation and lyricism exist for their own sake in his writing. His writing has influenced the reader for the acceptance of environmental advocacy.

Nature-responsiveness is a kind of culture or rather counter culture. One must pursue it to resist the homocentrism. Nature responsiveness determines one's psychological and social worlds. Lopez argues that humble aspiration of environmental mimesis is far healthier for an individual, and for a society, than the arrogance of cyberspace.

John Burroughs, late nineteenth century essayist, naturalist, and critic, credits "the true poet with greater insight into nature than the naturalist" in his essay, "Nature and the Poets." He believed that the greater the poet, the more correct and truthful will be his specifications.

George Eliot, the greatest of all Victorian novelists, praised Ruskin's doctrine, in a review of the third volume of *Modern Painters*:

> All truth and beauty are to be attained by a humble and faithful study of nature, and not by substituting vague forms...in place of definitive, substantial reality. Eliot acknowledged that the thorough acceptance of this doctrine would remould our life; and who teaches its application to any one department of human activity with such power as Mr. Ruskin's, is a prophet for his generation.

Each of Thoreau's four books, centers on a simple excursion or a series of excursions: *A Week on the Concord and Merrimack Rivers*, on a two-week trip to the White Mountains of New Hampshire; *Walden*, on two years of bivouacking at the pond; *The Maine Woods*, on three journeys to Maine reported successively; and *Cape Cod*, on three trips to Cape Cod.

Nature is a mirror of moral health. Emerson's environmental achievements are great. Nature took great stride toward philosophic or theological naturalism. If everyone possesses the great degree of environmental sensitivity, there would be no environmental problems. The problems of pollution, resource depletion, species eradication have become consistently serious. These dangers are rapidly increasing. Environmental texts are the transforming agents to quicken or produce an environmentalist commitment. Thoreau has produced environmentalist commitment through his works.

Thoreau chides his audience for their ignorance to nature. He had a deeply personal love and reverence for nature like Muir. It is the basis for a more enlightened environmental ethic and polity.

Lawrence Buell explored the environmental perception, the place of nature in the history of western thought. He imagines a more ecocentric way of being. Henry Thoreau is the most frequent reference point.

Thoreau's *Walden* is the central book in the green American thinking. Thoreau is the unique representative of green American thinking. Buell explicated the American environmental imagination.

If as environmental philosophers contend, western metaphysics and ethics need revision before we can address today's environmental problems, then environmental crisis involves a crisis of the imagination the amelioration of which depends on better ways of imaging nature and humanity's relation to it.

Environmental interpretation requires us to rethink our assumptions about the nature of representation, reference, metaphor, characterization, personae, and canonicity. Albert Gore pronounced anxiety about the environment strongly. Since 1970 there has been continued discussion about the need to set limits to techno economic growth. Environmentalism is certainly one of the catalysts for the formation of global culture. Creative and critical arts are clearly exercising, however, unconsciously, an influence upon the emerging culture of environmental concern. They have also played a significant role in shaping every other aspect of human culture.

How we image a thing, true or false, affects our conduct toward it, the conduct of nations as well as persons. Aesthetics is a decisive force for or against environmental change. Literary creations in Denmark infused erstwhile desolate heathlands with meaning and potential.

Awareness of the potential gravity of environmental degradation among the people should result in the effective care of the nature. We must translate perception for the environment into effective action. Our perceptions about the environment must be powerful to maintain the ecological balance. E.O. Wilson warned that, "No intellectual vice is more crippling than defiantly self-indulgent anthropocentrism." Buell believed strongly that pastoral ideology is central to American cultural self-understanding. The key figure of the American literary renaissance of the mid-nineteenth century is Thoreau. The writings of Susan Fenimore Cooper are significant. Aldo Leopold's formation of biocentric environmental ethics was important. In the Cold War era, ecocide was always a more serious threat than nuclear destruction. In literary history the resurgence of environmental writing is as important as the rise of magical realist fiction. An environmentally oriented work spreads ethical values. Human history is implicated in natural history.

A human being should have ecological consciousness. Urbanization wrought social displacement. It links the natural, human, and divine estates. It has serious, contemplative and reverential tone.

Place

In the ancient and modern creative writing sense of place is of great significance. Place ought to be central in the theory of environmental imagination. Wendell Berry said, "In the moral (the ecological) sense you cannot know until you have learned where." Berry celebrates self-conscious commitment to place which produces environmental responsiveness. Environmental humility, an awakened place-awareness makes one conscious that 'place moulds us as well as vice versa.'

Environmental non-fiction has the variegated, striking character. *Walden* belongs to many genres. One can read it as a poem, a novel, an autobiography, a travel narrative, a sermon, a treatise. Environmental non-fiction is more heteroglossic than that of the novel.

Environmental non-fiction is an important literary enterprise. Nature has become a centrally important subject for creative prose. Prose writers in Britain have made Nature a central subject in their writing with more activism. The interrelated developments of modernisation, romanticist aesthetics, and popular natural history in Britain were ahead of America. Thoreau read seriously the book about nature was William Howitt's *The Book of the Seasons* (1831). Howitt aimed to respiritualise an increasingly commercial people through restitution of contact with nature. One's nature influence is implanted. He wrote for the urban bourgeois. The book excites a spirit of attachment to nature. He creates a meticulously objective and subjective account of seasonal change and phenomena. The book promotes moral transformation. Emerson's *Nature* has become a literary classic. Thoreau's book *Walden* is not the first book to deal with local travels.

Washington Irving presented the native tales in *The Sketchbook* (1817). Mary Russell Mitford, British author created ambitious *Our Village* (1824-1832). Walden draws on the Nature traditions. Susan Fenimore Cooper wrote *Rural Hours* (1850). *Rural Hours* is the first major work of American literary bioregionalism. She exhibits a finely celebrated environmental sense. Cooper writes out of a passionate attachment to her locale combined with distress and contempt for provincialism. She seeks to correct provincialism through practicality, erudition, and assertion. She directs some of her sharpest thrusts against ignorance of nature. She wrote in another work, "we are still…half aliens to the country Providence has given us." It was Cooper, not Thoreau, who among all antebellum writers wrote the most comprehensive short treatise on the history of environmental consciousness in world cultures from ancient times to the present. Cooper takes delight in natural over artificial charms. She was consciously in touch with the literary world. Theory of landscape representation has moved in a more realist direction.

Darwin achieved a breakthrough in Victorian prose by expressing through his rhetoric the vision of the delicacy of formal categories that constitute the revolutionary element of his philosophy of evolution. Darwin's ideas and Thoreau's art have influenced the course of modern science and modern environmental writing respectively. They have also exerted influence on the rewriting of history.

Thoreau was an attentive reader in the field of landscape aesthetics. His favorite form of environmental prose, travel narratives appealed to more than any other kind of contemporary writing. Darwin brought together the natural and human phenomena. He made observations together of *Homo sapiens* non-human species, and landscape panoramas. Boundaries between species become porus in the reading experience.

> A large intellectual gap exists between our sense of being actors in the world, of always being in place, and the "placelessness" that characterize our attempts to theorise about human actions and events.[4] (J. Nicholas Entrikin, *The Betweenness of Place*)

Lawrence Buell focused on art's capacity to image and remythify the natural environment. Pastoral both satirized and replicated the hypercivilization of urban life. Pastoralism is a species of cultural equipment.

American literature has been preoccupied with country and wilderness as setting, theme, and value in contradiction to society and the urban. It has also represented the sociological facts of urbanization and industrialization. Jeffersonianism has made an impact on American literature. Jefferson's *Notes on the State of Virginia* is written on the eve of industrial revolution. He offered an agrarian vision in it. Nature is one of the pre-eminently formative influences in traditional if not in contemporary American writing. It is a positive cultural value. Social prophets have envisioned that a society founded on the order of nature will be free from corruption.

Environmental deterioration has become too obvious to ignore. Physical nature is a touchstone of value for the instruction of one's culture. Pastoral is enlisted as a vehicle of national self-definition. Nature is not just the theatre of human actions but nature exists for its own sake. Technologised culture insulates one from the natural environment and splits one's allegiances. Modern environmentalists who speak for the green world are contemporary new world pastoralists. Emerson and Thoreau criticized the hypercivilised effeteness of Boston.

People must inhabit their environment responsibly. They have to perceive it something other than just a green world, a dream, a concept. The environment we inhabit is poisoned. People should learn to use productive environment in the interest of humanity and earth's interest. Many environmental thinkers have suggested the need for new paradigms for envisioning the relation between human and non-human. Freya Mathews presented a new paradigm in *The Ecological Self*. Neil Evernden wrote *The Social Creation of Nature*. He argues that a reinvention of vision and values is the key to environmental amelioration. We should begin to look beyond the mythical vision as well as through it to assume the responsibility of the environment. Eighteenth century intellectuals like Jefferson and Timothy Dwight formulated America's identity and promise in term of ruralist myth of provincial virtue. It is opposed to an increasingly overpopulated, citified, industrialising Europe. Many American writers have celebrated the landscape grandeur in America through their works.

Timothy Dwight and Washington Irving are the pioneers in the genre of the village sketch. It is also known as local colorism. Virtue tends to correlate with rurality even when rurality includes poverty, gloom and intolerance.

Indigenes have used pastoral for serving their own counter hegemonic ends. They have used pastoral as a weapon against cultural dominance. We find some outstanding examples in Native American literature. Leslie Mermon Silko criticizes mainstream civilization in *Ceremony*. He presents an updated version of traditional native wisdom.

Sense of place is necessarily always a social product. George Eliot praised Ruskin in a review of third volume of *Modern Painters*, "doctrine that all truth and beauty are to be attained by a humble and faithful study of nature, and not by substituting vague forms...in place of definite, substantial reality." Eliot affirmed that a thorough acceptance of this doctrine, would remould our life; and who teaches its application to any one department of human activity with such power as Mr. Ruskin's, is a prophet for his generation.

> The unit of survival is an organism-in-its environment. If the environment fails to survive, so does the individual.[5]
> (Freya Mathews, *The Ecological Self*)

Lawrence Buell has written *Writing for an Endangered World: Literature, Culture, and Environment in the U.S. and Beyond*. This is the second book written by Buell about environmental imagination. His previous book, *The Environmental Imagination* dealt with forms of literary imagination. According to him environmental crisis is not merely one of economic resources, public health, and political deadlock. Sustained public support for environmental policy will safeguard environment of the country. He has presented a coherent vision of environment. Sociologist Ulrich Beck remarked about debates over species extinction: "Only if nature is brought into people's everyday images, into stories they tell, can its beauty and its suffering be seen and focused on." The success of all environmentalist efforts finally hinges not on technology or science but on a state of mind: on attitudes, feelings, images, narratives.

Classic texts and genres continue to exert influence. Sumerian epic Gilgamesh is an allegory of settlement culture's triumph over hunter gatherer culture, town over forest. The worlds' physical environment is being increasingly refashioned by capital, technology, and geopolitics. Non-human world is important for the preservation of life. He believes that reorientation of human attention and values according to a stronger ethic of care for the nonhuman environment would make the world a better place, for humans as well as non-humans. Anthropocentric concerns such as public health and environmental equity are motivators of environmental imagination and commitment. Political and economic enfranchisement guarantees heath, safety and sustenance. We should pursue genuinely alternative paths of development to achieve modest environmental reforms. Fears for survival of family and self are more powerful motivators than care for nature. Thoreau, a green saint, acknowledged four basic material necessities, food, fuel, clothing, shelter. The environmental crisis threatens all landscapes—wild, rural, suburban, and urban. Physical environment is the indispensable shaping force in human art, experience and such aesthetic works. Attachment to place is a creative force. Environmental connectedness requires acts of imagination at three stages: in the bonding, in the telling, in the understanding. Physical environment is a ground of personal and social identity.

Franklin imagines a new urban ecological order. Franklin's *Autobiography* is an early republican literary classic. William Bertram wrote *Travels in Florida*. He seeks to activate environmental perception to the end of social improvement. He described individual species of plants and animals. Environmental sensitivity is basic to human psycho physiological composition. "Ecological identity" is a holistic term. People construe themselves in different ways in relationship to the earth as manifested in personality, values, actions, and sense of self.

Attachment to a place is a creative force. One should respect for the physical environment. The success of environmental efforts does not depend on some technology or new science; it depends on attitudes, feelings, images, narratives. Power of imagination brings wonders in human life. Sociologist Ulrich Beck remarked about species extinction: "only if nature is brought into people's everyday images, into the stories they tell, can its beauty and its suffering be seen and focused on."

Human beings are biohistorical creatures; they construct themselves in interaction with surroundings. Nature culture distinction itself is an anthropocentric product. It comes from the change from nomadism to settlement that began millennia ago in southwestern Asia. Capital, technology, and geopolitics have refashioned physical environment. To achieve environmentalism, we must follow alternative paths: rejection of consumer society, communitarian anti-modernism, animal liberation. Jonathan Bate affirms, “the dream of deep ecology will never be realized upon the earth, but our survival as a species may be dependent on our capacity to dream it in the work of our imagination.” The environmental crisis threatens all landscapes—wild, rural, suburban, and urban. Greenhouse effect has endangered the places. Ecocritics acknowledge that physical environment is the vital force in human art, experience and aesthetic works. Buell argues that a comprehensive public land policy must address both human needs and ecosystem imperilment. Efficient management of the physical environment is crucial to human and social health. Imagination is a preservative against the confusion of the world. Environmental connectedness requires acts of imagination at three stages: bond, expression, and understanding. Physical environment is a central floor of personal and social identity. Human experience is formed in transaction with nature.

Benjamin Franklin, William Bertram seeks to activate environmental perception to the aim of social improvement. If people are environmentally unconscious, it is impossible for them to come to complete consciousness at whatever level: observation, thought, articulation etc. The power of imagination can achieve breakthroughs. Literary artists deal with the environmental unconscious in aspects, occluding and enabling. According to Lawrence Buell, embeddedness in physical context is constitutive of personal and social identity.

Chapter I, “Toxic Discourse,” deals with the rhetoric and ethics of imagined endangerment. Toxic discourse is culturally significant. People have become aware of the hazards of the poisoned world. Medicine, political science, history, sociology, economics, and ethics have contributed to the debate of the fear of a poisoned world. Anxiety arises from perceived threat of environmental hazard due to chemical modification by human agency. Thought, values, feeling, expression, and persuasion may be more influential in the remediation of environmental problems than the instruments of technology and politics.

Ecocriticial movement has brought the issues of environment within literary and rhetorical studies.

Environmental justice affirms the sacredness of mother earth. All species are interdependent. Every species has the right to be free from ecological destruction. Environmentalism is an instrument of social justice. The fear of environmental poisoning has made environmentalism a compelling public issue. Environmental crisis endangers public health. "A healthy environment is necessary for a healthy economy" (*Environmental Values in American Culture,* p. 257). Human cooperation and respect is necessary for life and well-being. Rachel Carson introduced toxic discourse effectively in *Silent Spring* (1962). Leo Marx in *The Machine in the Garden* discussed the techno-economic progress to which national policy has always been committed with escapist fantasies of inexhaustible natural beauty. Creative artists envision communities of safe, clean, ample residential and public spaces. Carson insists: "every human being is now subjected to contact with dangerous chemicals from the moment of conception until death." Communities are contaminated with the occult toxic networks. Public policies and power makes vital impact on the health and quality of the individual human life. George Perkins Marsh presented an image of a ruined world in *Man and Nature* (1864). Environmental reform is linked with social justice.

Chapter II, "The Place of Place," focuses on place attachment as a resource in the articulation of environmental unconscious. Human beings are located somewhere, in particular locations. Environment is not something different from us. Environment is part of our being. Edward Casey affirms: "a placeless world is as unthinkable as a bodiless self." The novel, *Gain* suggests colonizing force of transnational capitalism. Toxification practices of the multinational corporations manifest through its impact-emotional as well as physical on bodies and families. Contemplating the impact of Toxification on the people, people can question the patterns of hegemony. Place has multiple dimensions, it is significant for the maintenance of the culture. Environmental endangerment or environmental well-being can be properly understood if one possesses a keen sense of place.

During the last quarter of the twentieth century place has reappeared in humanistic and social theory as a term of analysis. Sense of place makes us capable to understand the oneness of human and non-human. The sense of place is inevitable in nationalism. Place is associated with ethnic, political, informational, cultural and religious formations. Native American novelist Leslie Silko beautifully expressed the delicacy of place in *Ceremony* (1977). He is faithful to the intricacy of the web of relations and feelings that comprises a deep sense of place. He has brought environmental unconscious to full articulation. Place sense is important to literary and cultural imagination. Places shape the personal identity; cultural artifacts also reshape the personality. The power of image is key to which makes individuals and people feel place connected. Our experience of the natural world is always reshaped by rhetorical constructs like photography, industry and advertising. Institutions like religion, tourism and education form the sense of place. Visual and other information technologies can enhance place sense. Some of the places that move us deeply even though we have seen them only in the mind's eye are actual places. Without benefit of this, our sense of world citizenship might suffer. We feel the sense of accountability for suffering in Bosnia, Somalia, Rwanda, and Kosovo. Certain imagined places that have moved people deeply are more purely visionary, like the traditional image of heaven or hell. The imagined celestial city sought by the protagonist Christian in John Bunyan's Pilgrim's Progress moves people deeply. Centuries of writers have described the place of heaven and believers have visualized it.

Place imagination plays a crucial role in human life. It is universal compulsion for human beings to seek to connect themselves with places of settlement. Loss of sense of place produces pathological effects like insomnia, affective disorder. A person who does not feel placelessness as loss, there is something deeply wrong with that person. Kentucky regionalist writer Wendell Berry puts it:

> How you act should be determined, and the consequences of your acts are determined, by where you are. To know where you are (and whether or not that is where you should be) is at least as important as to know what you are doing, because in the moral (the ecological) sense you cannot know what until you have learned where. Not knowing where you are, you can lose your soul or your soil, your life or your way home.[6] (*Standing by Words,* p. 103)

Place sense teaches how to live well in a place. Leslie Silko affirmed that she wrote *Ceremony* to recreate her home place in compensation for absence from it. The novel imagines the psychic reintegration of the protagonist Tayo largely as a matter of reintegration with place. Phenomenologist David Abram wrote a book full of insights about place, *The Spell of the Sensuous*. He remarks:

> In the oral, indigenous world, to tell certain stories without saying precisely where those events occurred (or if one is recounting a vision or dream, to neglect to say where one was when granted the vision), may alone render the telling powerless or ineffective. (David Abram, p. 182)

Place affects well-being through physical environment, social context, and phenomenology of perception. Place connectedness maximizes well-being. Connection to soil is surely not the whole measure of one's spiritual health. Place attachment can create possessiveness, ethnocentrism, and racial intolerance. Place-centeredness can make one vulnerable outside one's place. If people are ecologically ignorant or possessive, they may be dangerous to the place. Place is more deeply a matter of belonging than possession. Space should be converted or reconverted into place. Place is outside the range of vision of people.

Chapter three, "Flaneur's Progress: Reinhabiting the City" is about reassessment of the urban writing. He examines the Woolf, and various other writers. He explicated the perception of metropolis as an ecocultural habitat. He criticizes self-protective autonomy of the urban people. People have been hurt by ecological illiteracy. People must relearn what it means to be native to a place. Reorientation process is not a solitary quest. It involves the engagement with a place's human and non-human environment. Place attachment molds one's identity.

Wendell Berry, John Elder, Gary Snyder rediscovered their respective places, Kentucky, Green Mountain village life, and California. Frederick Law Olmsted is the best known American exemplar of green city thinking. The contemporary bioregionalism has influenced the central insight of the urban planners. Sale affirms: "every city is part of a region, and depends on the surrounding countryside for many of its resources and much of its market, and every city is built upon a natural foundation." Natural landscape is transformed as urban-industrial place. Physical environment constitutes the urban landscape.

Charles Dickens and Walt Whitman were the first major creative writers who studied the city deeply and portrayed in literary works. Whitman was an ardent admirer of Dickens. He animated the democratic ideal of equability and fraternity. Whitman's poetry deals with the urban world of strangers. He wrote about New York, a city of extraordinary wealth and power, and equally remarkable for pollution, diseases. He said that environmental negligence, and injustice contributes to worse problems of dirt, pollution, disease, uncontrolled growth, and overcrowding. He crusaded against unhealthy and unsafe working conditions. He campaigned through his newspaper for new water and sewer systems for the city of Brooklyn. Both, Charles Dickens and Walt Whitman express commitment to the ideal of a city sweet and clean. Whitman believed that social reform is not brought by institutional change but bringing about amendment of behaviour through change reflected in attitudes. He insists on contact with landscape and others. Urban inhabitant should not be self-absorbed. He knew that inhabitants of the city should be more mutually trusting. Consciousness and identity are continually shaped and reshaped through interaction with the people and nature.

Joyce imagines the city as a compatible habitat. Bloom remembers the song about praising of country life and celebrating community. Joyce expressed the desire to connect with environment through Bloom. He gave a complete picture of Dublin. He created urban consciousness through Bloom. Public and private interpenetrate.

Virginia Woolf described postwar London in *Mrs. Dalloway*. She presented a more dominant cityscape. She is exceptionally sensitive to the vibrations of environmental unconscious in molding the human life. She believed that urban life could be made aesthetic. She described the interplay between physical stimuli and mental life. Woolf perceives Personhood develops through confluence of people with each other and with physical environment, each shaping the other simultaneously. William Carlos Williams expressed perceptions of bioregionalism through poetry. He had refined urban ecological imagination. He created exciting pictures of urban landscapes. Nature asserts itself. He created poems faithful to the place. He creates an ecopoetics of the city. He displayed a keen sense of ecological relationships. Urban centers depend on environmental circumstances which are rarely noticed by the city dwellers. City is a natural habitat. City is a part of the ecosystem.

Chapter one to three are about mixed signals to the degree to which people and communities should be seen as constructed by place. Chapter four, "Discourses of Determinism" reviews nineteenth and twentieth century writers and their creative works which reveal lives place determined. Reinhabitation comprises a voluntary sense of place. Toxic discourse states people may be more entrapped than they think in a place more dangerous than they think. People's lives are inevitably emplaced. Biogeographically human destinies are influenced. Environment shapes people more than they shape it. Socialist theory believes that human collective can change society. Modernization reinforces faith in human power to control environment.

From Herodotus to Montesquieu, creative artists have contemplated that character has often been produced by location. Circumstance constructs character and behaviour. Public health theory has avowed that dirt and bad housing is responsible for epidemic disease. Creative writers have probed the notion that inheritance or environment determines human communities.

Charles Dickens was the first major creative writer in the English language who explores the modern urban problems in fictional works. He presented individual differences in great cities. He described the sense of the city impressing itself on people for better or worse. Dickens later novels reproduce houses, neighborhoods, factories, landscapes as scenes of confinement. Stephen Blackpool in *Hard Times* (1854) finds prison of his whole adult life within the midlands factory town. *Bleak House* demonstrates the interdependence of people and the environment. Dickens constructs psychic landscapes true to the urban environment. Miller Confirms, "Nature is buried behind a thick surface of roads, streets, buildings, signs, values, meanings" (Miller, p. 295).

Charles Dickens' *Little Dorrit* represents environmental determinism. He described social parasitism and literal pollution in London. The sanitary condition of the neighborhood predicts the inhabitant's state of well-being. Clean environment ensures both bodily and mental health.

Upton Sinclair's *The Jungle* (1906) projects the Lithuanian immigrant family who bought the property too quickly. At first sight family members thought it is their dream house. Later they realized it is too literal overpriced. The house was built on a former garbage dump. They suffered a ghastly odor of dead things. In the place one never saw fields or any green thing whatever. Factory smoke blackened the air above and swarms blackened the air below.

Emile Zola described in *Germinal* the reducing of the people to pawns, workers to tools. Escape becomes unimaginable for the characters from the confinement of working places.

Richard Wright rendered entrapment of the people starkly in the naturalist novel, *Native Son* (1940). He deals with the sensuous feel of urban blight. Many people get sick and die in slum living conditions. He described the conditions in which Negroes lived. He was acquainted with poverty and discrimination He identified himself with the protagonist in *Native Son*. He affirmed the misery, alienation, potentiality for violence of any native son. Native son live among the greatest possible plenty on earth but he cannot get access to it. He presented the mechanization of human life under harsh working conditions and stress.

Rurality is the fate of human life. Environment constructs human identity. Nature and culture are the interdependent determiners of human life. The Speaker in Wordsworth's poem "Tintern Abbey" affirms, "Nature never did betray/ the heart that loved her." Natural harmony is not only a fact nut it is also a value. Wordsworth wrote about the predicament of the people in rural surroundings.

Transaction with the natural environment determines the health of persons and communities. Nature can have constructive as well as blighting influence on human life. Ethical-political commitment is the determiner of the human and non-human relationships. Homogeneous community exhibits healthy relationship with nature.

Jane Addams wrote magnificent essay, "A Modern Lear." Industry in principle is or ought to be like family. She has described the irony of self-serving manipulator. She resisted arrogant imposition of limits decided by political leaders. People are always place-bound whether they know it or not. Physical nature, human nature, or socio-culture are the primary determiners of human life. Ethical-political commitment constitutes human life. Environment is a precondition for elementary human dignity and accomplishment.

Chapter five, "Modernization and the Claims of the Natural World: Faulkner and Leopold" describes the relationship between human community and non-human and its place-connectedness. William Faulkner and Aldo Leopold developed ethics of land stewardship through their creative works.

Human beings should behave ethically with the non-human. To become reinhabitor to a place and the awakening of a sense of environmental determinism requires reconceiving the human relation to the non-human and to extend ethical values to them. We should be compassionate to animals and trees. Pre-industrial cultures lived in closer symbiosis with nature than we do. A determinist approach tends minimize difference between human beings and animals as environmental constraints affect both equally. A reinhabitor thinks compassionately of animals. An environmental determinist thinks humans and non-humans in the same boat.

A lively sense of mentality contemplates scenes of rapid environmental change. Many writers' creative works have been influenced by the experience or knowledge of environmental change. James Fennimore Cooper's Cooperstown novel, *The Pioneers,* and his daughter, Susan Fenimore Cooper's literary daybook Rural Hours, Thoreau's *Walden*, George Perkins Marsh's *Man and Nature* reflect deeper understanding of nature. William Faulkner has reflected environmental ethic through his novels. Leopold and Faulkner were disconcerted by ruthless exploitation of rurality by industry and agribusiness. Both of them reconceived the place of nature within the space of culture.

William Faulkner is an environmental historian. His interest in environmental change was one dimension of his interest in southern character and history. The material distinctiveness of regional environment is basic to his depiction of place. Sense of future shock wrought by technological innovation is the core of his first important Yoknapatawpha fiction, *Flags in the Dust*. He takes insightful account of southern modernization, especially its casualties and failures. He connects people to landscape. The plot of *Light in August* intertwines forest history with social history. The workers in the mill are underpaid. They lived in a nondescript house. They obtained the plainest of food and clothing. Few were ever able to rise in the economic and social scale. They had no ambition. They were satisfied with living in the present. They were not concerned with the future of themselves or their children. All the characters are what they are not just because of who they are. But history of Mississippi has influenced lives of the people. Lucas's placelessness becomes a stalking horse for his partner Joe Christmas's more extreme placelessness. It is a product of his culture's shortsightedness about natural resources. For Joe Christmas, it is a product of the culture's shortsightedness about race.

Environmental history illuminates Faulkner's fiction. Faulkner was a natural historian. He exhibited mature aesthetics to infuse truth with myth, legend, and poetic rhetoric. He has interwoven characters with the environmental realism. *Light in August* reflects surrealistic image of the blighted landscape. It is the contemporary vision of nature and its impact on human beings.

Gerard Manly Hopkins assured the regeneration of nature. Faulkner's profuse description of nature should have influenced the magical realism of Gabriel Garcia Marquez and other Latin American novelists. Natural forces assert themselves. Faulkner made the strongest presentation of nature untrammeled in *Go Down, Moses* (1942). He was committed for natural reflection. *Go Down, Moses* is the description of the relationship between the people of white and black race. It also foregrounds environmental reflection. Fate of the character is linked to the fate of character. He dramatized environmental consciousness.

Aldo Leopold is known as the father of modern environmental ethics. *A Sand Country Almanac* is the most enduring work written by Leopold. It is about land ethic. Leopold states that all species have a right to exist as a matter of biotic right. He emphasised that human beings should treat nature properly. From twenty-first-century perspective non-human creatures should be regarded as moral agents. Leopold asserts, "It is only the scholars who understands why the raw wilderness gives definition and meaning to the human enterprise" (*A Sand Country Almanac,* pp. 200-01).[7] They attempted to instill respect for the natural world. They enhanced aesthetics of environmental perception. Faulkner wrote with considerable knowledge of southern environmental history and its economic, social and racial ramifications. He is the harbinger of southern environmentalism. Leopold is rhetoric in the writing of nature. Faulkner presented psychohistorical case studies through fictional works. He explored split allegiances, self-deception, and ironic unintended consequences. *Go Down, Moses* is an unusually rich meditation in environmental ethics. Faulkner constructs a complicated ethical dilemma around environmental doublethink: the experience of being caught between one's environmentalist propensities and the inertial drag of selfish values. One's commitment to something is always muddled by other commitments, distractions, or sheer inanity. Faulkner exposes the chuckleheadedness of his wilderness lovers: their inability to think straight about wilderness issues.

Chapter six "Global Commons as Resource and as Icon: Imagining Oceans and Whales" is about the appropriate regulation of economic development so that the natural resources and environmental quality will not be degraded. The risk society paradigm puts the globe under the sign of toxic endangerment. United Nations report *Our Common Future* promotes sustainable development.

Rachel Carson wrote the most significant book of the sea in the nature writing tradition, *The Sea Around Us* (1950). She has told the toxic effects of DDT and other chemical pesticides. She focused on the anthropogenic degradation of the island biogeography. Literature and the discourses of cultural production should offer insight and commitment for the protection of nature and human life.

Chapter seven "The Misery of Beasts and Humans: Non-anthropocentric Ethics versus Environmental Justice" is about ethics and aesthetics. Mahasweta Devi's Bengali novella translated by Gayatri Spivak in 1995, "Pterodactyl, Puran Sahay, and Pirtha" is an environmental justice fiction. Pirtha is a small village. Exploitative deforestation has accelerated evaporation, erosion which have deteriorated soil quality. Pterodactyl symbolizes tribal identity. Pirthans themselves have become demoralized. Villager's plight is linked with the plight of the non-human world.

Chapter eight "Watershed Aesthetics" explicates the important role of water in human life. Without water life is not possible. Civilizations have been defined by the rivers throughout the world. Rivers are local, regional and national signifiers.

Charles Booth exposed monumental poverty through *Darkest England* (1890). According to Leopold, humans and non-humans peacefully co-exist in the biotic community. Each activity of life-form depends on the shared supply of water. Watershed writing respect environmental health, equity and self-restraint.

Lawrence Buell has written *The Future of Environmental Criticism: Environmental Crisis and Literary Imagination* in 2005. He presented endangered state and uncertain fate of life on earth. According to W.E.B. Du Bois, the environmental crisis is a major question in the twenty-first century. He has discussed the emergence of ecocriticism, environmental imaging and representation, reconception of place as a fundamental dimension of both art and life, its string, ethical and political commitment.

Literary and cultural studies has got environmental turn in the 1990s. Ecocriticism is a heterogeneous movement. Creative art and critical reflection have always taken a keen interest in how the material world is engaged, absorbed and reshaped by theory, imagination and technology. Environmental discourse is rooted in ancient times. Mayan mythography symbolizes the collective survival that must exist between humans, plants, and animals. The chapter first in the book reviews the appearance of a new critical theory, "The Emergence of Environmental Criticism."

Environmental criticism is an emergent discourse. It is one with very ancient roots. It corrects the marginalization of environmental issues in versions of critical theory that dominated literary and cultural studies through the 1980s. Setting in the novel or drama is not merely the backdrop of human actions. Egdon Heath, the non-human entity is the main character in Thomas Hardy's *The Return of the Native.* Thoreau's *Walden,* Rachel Carson's *Silent Spring, The Sea Around Us* describe the strong bond between humanity and nature. Now environment has taken the hold of public concern worldwide. Kenyan environmental activist, Wangari Maathai has been awarded the Nobel Peace Prize in 2004. Modern industrial society is incapable to manage its unintended environmental consequences. Ulrich Beck proposed the contemporary theory that even the privileged classes of the world inhabit a global "risk society." Hazards cannot be anticipated, calculated, and controlled, much less escaped (Beck, Giddens, and Lash 1994: 6; cf. Beck 1986; Williams 2004).

Environmental issues have become an increasing provocation for artists and academics. Cross-disciplinary environmental studies programmes have become very attractive within colleges and universities. Teaching and scholarship have become environmentally directed. Issues of vision, value, culture, and imagination are keys to today's environmental crises. Humans should become the part of the biotic community. Human beings are ecologically embedded. Ecocriticism attempts to solve the problem of humankind's alienation from nature. It questions the concepts, on which the old hierarchies are built, androcentrism, anthropocentrism. The term implies the methodological holism. It has been more aesthetic, ethical, and socio-political than scientistic.

The Beginnings of Ecocriticism

The term ecocriticism was coined by Rueckert in 1970s. Ralph Waldo Emerson's *Nature* (1836) is the first canonical work of US literature to unfold a theory of nature. Leo Marx's *The Machine and the Garden: Technology and the Pastoral Ideal in American Culture* (1964). Raymond Williams' *The Country and the City* (1973) has been praised as a masterpiece of ecocriticism. Williams and Marx identified national essence symbolically with nature. They have explicated the irreversible transformation of landscape wrought by economic power and/or interest. They believed that the process of modernisation, industrial capitalism triumphed over pastoral and traditional local life. Williams described the endangered country folk and the culture of rural country folk. Peasant poet, John Clare and regional novelist, Thomas Hardy wrote faithfully about the nature and rural life. Ecocriticism takes the cognizance of humanity's ongoing interaction with "the non-human forces in which our lives are embedded" (Hess, 2004: 77, 95).

Ecocritics read environmental imagination as a barometer of national imagination. Joseph Meeker's *The Comedy of Survival* (1972, revd. 1997) is considered as the starting point for American ecocriticism. Williams and Bate are committed to the ethical values as the part of contemporary structure of values.

The first wave ecocriticism deals environment as natural environment. Ecological criticism aims to struggle to preserve the biotic community. It studied the effects of culture on nature. It celebrates nature. It redefines the term culture in organist term. It removes the separation between human life and other elements of nature. Buell's *The Environmental Imagination* is the representative work of first wave of ecocriticism. Social criticism treats urban and degraded landscapes as seriously as natural landscapes. Personhood can be understood in the context of nature.

Native American writer quoted by an Ecocritic/nature writer has explained the strong connection of humanity with nature: "You could cut off my hand, and I would still live.... You could take out my eyes, and I would still live...take away the sun, and I die. Take away the plants and animals, and I die. So why should I think my body is more a part of me than the sun and the earth?" (K.D. Moore, 2004: 58-59). Environment is crucial to health or disease, life or death on planet earth. First wave of ecocriticism breaks down the hierarchical separations between human beings and other elements of nature.

Second wave ecocriticism presents nature within cities. It exposes crimes of eco-injustice against marginal groups within the society. Ecocriticism is committed to the nature protection ethic. It is also committed to the environmental justice. It also exposes eco-injustice against marginal groups within the society. Terry Tempest Williams and Sandra Steingraber have written about metropolitan environmental cancer clusters.

According to Lance Newman, "Nature writing is not a stable form of reaction to a stable problem. It is the dynamic response to the rise and development of the capitalist ecosocial order... how nature writers see and understand nature has everything to do with how they see and understand nature has everything to do with how they see and understand the society whose relations with it they hope to change" (Newman, 2002: 18-19). To understand ecocentric consciousness, one should possess historic consciousness. Newman argues that nature writing is implicitly positions against material, social and natural systems that have produced the environmental crisis. Nature writing has become politicized after Carson. Ecocriticism has become a great intellectual, critical movement in the twenty-first century. Its reach is worldwide.

Environmental criticism is a wide-open movement. It has evolved as a critical theory with intellectual zest and activist edge. Nature writing is a not a static but dynamic tradition. It responds to the rise and development of the capitalist ecosocial order. Newman argues that to understand ecocentric consciousness requires a historical consciousness. Nature writing reflects the material, social, and natural systems that has produced the present crisis of environmental endangerment. Environmental criticism is a wide-open movement. It is still sorting out its premises and its powers. Its reach is increasingly worldwide. It has become an integral part of graduate and post-graduate studies in some major university literature departments. It is wide open to alliances with environmental writers, environmental activists, and extra-academic environmental educators.

Chapter second "The World, the Text, and the Ecocritic," reconceives place as a fundamental dimension of both art and human experience. Environmental criticism strives to make the notion of environment from abstraction to concrete. Literary texts show the environment and human interaction to it. *Silent Spring* is a classic of toxic non-fiction. Environmental criticism theorizes the relationship between humanity and the natural world. The experience of subaltern victims of environmental injustice is presented through literary text. There is a close relationship between the text and the world. But text is not a replica of the world. Text is an environmental representation. Genres and texts themselves are arguably ecosystems. Texts reproduce sociohistorical environments. Every text is environmentally embedded, from its germination to its reception. A text may be environmentally unconscious, as one may be politically unconscious.

Rhetoric comprehends all genres of expression, literary, academic or popular. Environmental critics are strongly interested in rhetoric. We acquire the knowledge through language about the nature. All artistic works depend upon the evocation of imagined worlds that may or may not bear a close resemblance to literal or historical environment. Literary texts evoke fictive environmentality. Ecocritics explore the literary text as the refractions of physical environments and human interaction with those environments. Both first-wave and revisionist seek to break down the division between creative writing, criticism, field based environmental studies, and environmental activism. Carson's *Silent Spring* is classic toxic non-fiction.

There is the increasing interest among the literary scholars in popular culture. Science fiction has taken a keen interest in ecology, in planetary endangerment, in environmental ethics, in humankind's relationship with the non-human world. Science fiction has dealt with the issue of environment potentially.

Eminent science fiction writer and environmentalist, Ursula LeGuin wrote quite masterful novel *Lathe of Heaven* (1971). It is a psychological realist fiction. The novel is an elegant reflection on the paradox of eco-apocalyptic discourse. The protagonist George Orr is afflicted by effective dreams. If he dreams an event that never happened, it does. He finds the isolation and burden of responsibility unbearable. The novel is an elegant reflection on the paradox of eco-apocalyptic discourse.

Karen Tei Yamashita's magical realist, *Through the Arc of the Rain Forest* (1990) is a whimsical romp. It's protagonist, Kazumasa, is a Japanese expatriate cyborg. We must save the world drama based on techno-gimmickry. Soyinka argues in *A Dance of the Forests,* high-rolling extraction, consumption, and waste, global capitalism and transnational forms of greed have been responsible for the ecological crisis. These novels are serious works of environmental representation.

Chapter third is titled, "Space, Place, and Imagination from Local to Global." Environmental criticism arises within and against the history of human modification of planetary space. Human modification of planetary space has greatly accelerated since the industrial revolution. Relationship between being and habitat is dialectical. Place is a requisite concept for ecological humanists.

There is the clear distinction between space and place, as geographical concepts. World history is a history of space becoming place. One's residence is not space but place. Walter said, "A place is seen, heard, smelled, imagined, loved, hated, feared, revered" (Walter 1988: 142). Modernisation has rendered place attachment obsolete. Scientific and technological revolutions have made place attachment nugatory.

Place is rightfully the primary term. Place offers the promise of a "Politics of resistance" against modernism's excesses. Malpus argues that "places are part of the source of our rational capacities from the very beginning" (Malpus 1999: 35; Preston 2003: 116). All knowledge is situated. Physical embeddedness is a central place in ecological criticism. Ecofeminist philosopher, Val Plumwood, cautions, "place sensitivity requires both emotional and critical approaches to place" (Plumwood 2002: 233). Heidegger emphasizes that one should live responsively within one's environment.

Wilderness is a relative term rather than an absolute term. Sally Carrighar and Douglas Peacock wrote remarkable autobiographies. They wrote about the recovery from trauma induced social dysfunction through contact with wild animals. In classic environmental writing, Thoreau's *Walden* shows the characteristic problem of imagining a life closer to nature. Nature and culture are not separable domains. They must be seen as supporting. We have the capacity to image earth holistically. Literary texts also narrate representation of endangered communities. A place can be as small as a corner of our kitchen or as big as the planet. A protected reserve is cared for. In the same manner, if every place on the earth is cared for, the heath of the planet and people might be secured. A good thing should not be taken too far.

People are interdependent with the land. Global warming is likely to pose threats for coastal and island nations. Placeness is not only conditioned but it is inherent. Place consciousness involves orientation in space. One also becomes attached to a place, by the power of imagination alone. Folk stories and epics create the sense of place among the people. The places haunt one's dreams. Places to some extent define one's character. Imaged places induce loyalty and longing. They influence national behaviour and the course of world affairs.

Contemporary Ecolocalism is concerned with the threats to the bounded community from the outside. Kentucky farmer poet Wendell Berry argues, "We have become a nation of urban nomads." For him regionalism means, "Local life aware of itself." People develop long-term commitment to their community. Berry said,

> Without a complex knowledge of one's place, and without the faithfulness to one's place on which such knowledge depends, it is inevitable that the place will be used carelessly, and eventually destroyed. (Berry 1972: 67-69)

Wordsworth was a poet of the Lake District. Dickens' environmental imagination operated more at the level of urban life in London. Elizabeth Gaskell's *North and South* is a major work of Victorian environmental fiction. She sketched village life and the polluted urban life. The concept of the bioregion is important in the environmental criticism. People have a long-term commitment to the place where they live. It is an attempt of greening city life. Urban areas sprang into existence, and most often continue to depend on environmental circumstances.

Bioregional awareness means more prudent and self-sufficient use of natural resources such that environmental and human quality will be maintained and improved with better human-human and human/non-human considerations. We should be aware of the environmental consequences of our lifestyle.

Modern urban arrangements should take into account the role of environment in the sustenance of human life and culture. James Joyce's *Ulysses* and Woolf's *Mrs. Dalloway* portray the distance from environment damages the cities holistically. Hardy's novel *Woodlanders* (1887), describe people's lives get traumatically disrupted or extinguished because of the unsustainable relationship with nature.

Graham Swift's regional novel, *Waterland* tells the long narration of the East Anglian fenlands as a series of reshaping of landscape and social arrangements. The bioregional horizon must extend beyond a merely local horizon. The local cannot be separated from translocal forces.

Richard Powers' novel, *Gain* (1998) dramatizes the contrast between traditional and newer conceptions of environmental scale. It exposes the impossibility of understanding locales without taking account the power of destabilizing macro-forces. Barry Lopez attempts an ecohistorical anatomy of the entire Alaskan and Canadian Arctic as a single complex bioregion.

Sociologist, Ulrich Beck, argues that industrial modernisation has permanently destabilised life on earth. Technology can no longer control the damage wrought by its own unintended consequences. Since Chernobyl, the culture of modernisation has entered into a second reflexive stage that Beck calls the "risk society." We should reconcile techno-economic advancement, human environmental welfare, and the limits of earth's resources.

Walcott's epic, *Omeros* is a poem about the island-nation of St. Lucia, the author's home place. He writes the challenges before the people. He narrates the divide between the educated, expatriated poet and the local life. He gives voice to the local life. *Omeros* is a migratory, global and world historical. It evokes a sense of place. It romanticizes traditional peasant culture.

Chapter fourth is entitled, "The Ethics and Politics of Environmental Criticism." Ecocriticism is usually energized by environmental concern. It is openly polemical. It explores the issue widely known as ecological crisis. It raises public consciousness about history, present state, and possible future of the environmental interdependencies between human and nonhuman. Two polarizations are: ecocentric or biocentric vs. anthropocentric. For ecocentrists health of physical environment is the first priority. Anthropocentric thinkers are concerned with social welfare of interhuman equity. Ecocriticism has ecocentric face. Environmental writers themselves affirm the environmental construction of their identity.

Aldo Leopold extends the conception of community "to include soils, waters, plants and animals." A biotic community, in which humankind is one of the species, are entitled to existence as a matter of biotic right. Environmental crisis is not solely an economic problem. Leopold argues for the preservation of integrity, stability, and beauty of the biotic community.

Arne Naess, Norwegian philosopher and activist, coined the term, "deep ecology." Ecocentric criticism has also been influenced by Martin Heidegger, French phenomenologists Gaston Bachelard and especially Maurice Merleau-Ponty. They focused more on the body emplaced than on the mind giving itself over to place of abode. Gandhi influenced highly Naess. The wide impact of various strands of South and East Asian philosophy, particularly Hinduism, Buddhism and Taoism, on environmental writers is remarkable. Ecocentric thinking is more like a scatter gram than a united front. All its strains define human identity not as free standing, but in terms of its relationship with the physical environment and/or non-human life forms.

Leopold's land ethic has been most important for advocates of nature preservation. His biotic community is avowedly ethical. Ecocentrism recognizes the inflexible interdependence that subsists between the human and the nonhuman. Naess made a distinction between deep ecology and shallow ecology. Shallow ecology is designed to enhance amenities for those already well off. The relation between the humanity and nature is not inherent but dependent. Deep ecology looks more persuasive ontologically and aesthetically. As ontology, deep ecology and ecocentrism can provide a needful corrective to modern culture's underrepresentation of the degree to which humanness is ecosystemically imbricated.

Ecophilosopher Freya Mathews puts it: "To represent us as anything less than so interconnected is in fact to misrepresent us to ourselves, and hence to interfere with our possibilities of self-realization". From this position, ethical and political positions can be deduced. Jonathan Bate cordoned off criticism from politics by saying that literary criticism should not spell out a programme of action for better environmental management. According to him criticism should present the harmonious ways of living on the earth. He said that ethical and political proposals should be scrutinized, when put to the test of realistic implementation. Aldo Leopold's *Sand Country Almanac* is a classic of modern environmental writing and of ecocentric environmental ethics. Leopold argues that the biotic community's welfare should be the standard of right conduct. He awakens sleeping "ecological conscience." He insists that the world must no longer be thought of as revolving around "us". Reconstructive ecotheology is more dramatic example than green aesthetics or green ethics. Thomas Berry expresses promises in his widely influential *The Dream of the Earth*:

> Humanity's reenchantment with the earth as a living reality is the condition for our rescue of the earth from the impending destruction that we are imposing upon it. To carry this out effectively we must now, in a sense, reinvent the human species within the community of life species. Our sense of reality and of value must consciously shift from an anthropocentric to a biocentric norm of reference.[8] (*The Dream of the Earth*, 21)

Harvard Centre for the Study of World Religions sponsored the project, "Religions of the World and Ecology." The study of indigenous faiths and great traditions of Hinduism, Islam, Christianity, Judaism, Buddhism helps to reorient towards green thinking. These religious traditions have emphasized the unity of human and non-human life. Jonathan Bate tells eloquently the role of literature in the establishment of close kinship between nature and human life:

> We cannot do without thought experiments and language experiments which imagine a return to nature, a reintegration of the human and the other. The dream of deep ecology will never be realized upon the earth, but our survival as a species may be dependent on our capacity to dream it in

the work of our imagination.[9] (*The Song of the Earth*, 37)

Deep ecology emphasizes on identification of self as fulfilled through its identification with nature. Deep ecology and Ecofeminism share the common view of our embeddedness in nature. Plumwood said: "The basic concept required for an appropriate ethic of environmental activism is not that of identity or unity of but that of solidarity which requires not just the affirmation of difference, but also sensitivity to the difference between positioning oneself with the other and positioning oneself as the other."

Humanity's relation to the non-human is always socially mediated. Considerations of human welfare and equity strongly influenced the settlement of environmental questions. Ecofeminism is closer to social ecology than deep ecology. Social ecology aspires to confront and ultimately eliminate capitalism and social hierarchy. Ecofeminism has brought a shift in ecocriticism. Ecofeminists have pushed environmental criticism toward substantive engagement with issues of environmental welfare, social and economic equity, racism, poverty and toxification. Ecofeminism seems to be the most dynamic movement within environmental criticism. It takes the ethics and politic of ecocriticism in a sociocentric direction.

American environmental writing effectively begins with Rachel Carson's *Silent Spring* not with Thoreau or Frost or even Leopold. Environmental justice is the important component in ecocriticism. Ecocriticism's greatest challenge in the first part of the twenty-first century is to address the question of environmental concern in nature writing, nature poetry, and wilderness narrative. Critical horizons need to be expanded. Academic study and environmental practice are interdependent.

First National People of Color Environmental Leadership summit held in Washington DC incorporates the provisions of sustenance of natural resources. The provision four states:

> Environmental justice affirms the fundamental right to political, economic, cultural and environmental self-determination of all peoples.

Upton Sinclair exposed gross mistreatment of suffering workers in the Chicago meatpacking industry. He focused on a particular family of Lithuanian victims, who get maimed or killed off one by one. Friedrich Engels' *Condition of the Working Class in England* (1845) is the classic documentary work. Edward Abbey's *Desert Solitaire* or Leslie Silko's *Ceremony* are about the subject of nuclear contamination of respective imagined places. Oliver Goldsmith's eighteenth-century poem *The Deserted Village* is a reflection on ecological refugeeism: "But times are altered; Trade's unfeeling train/ Usurp the land and dispossess the swain" (*The Deserted Village*, p. 7).

Thoreau's *Walden* is the most canonical text in environmental literary non-fiction. It reflects author's experiment in simplicity. It is an interesting inquiry in ecology and culture. Gadgil and Guha have written about environmental refugees, the multitudes of landless poor crowded into India's urban slums.

Ecocriticism' agenda is concerned with issues of social justice and equity. Environmental criticism in literature is moving beyond the arena of nature. It addresses the question of how natural and social environments impinge on each other. It expresses concern for the most essential needs of the humanity. The two concerns are inherently interwoven. It deals with the reconciliation of the human life and non-human life. Serious artists write about the future of humanity and earth both so must the critics do.

Chapter fifth is entitled, "Environmental Criticism's Future." Buell brings out that every critical movement faces certain challenges or crises which are four: The challenge of organization, the challenge of professional legitimation, and the challenge of establishing significance beyond academy. The progress of environmental criticism has been encouraging. The Association for the Study of Literature and Environment has become a worldwide network. Environmental criticism in literature and the arts clearly should get the standing within the academy of such other issue driven discourses as those of race, gender, sexuality, class, and globalisation. Ecocriticism has now become a part of graduate and post-graduate programmes in various parts of the world. Environmental history has assumed central status in its discipline. Environmental criticism has now got clear visibility and standing. An interest in the environmental issues has become a plus attribute for young academics in literature.

Environmental criticism has not changed literary studies or environmental humanities. It has been absorbed therein. It has introduced a fresh topic or perspective or archive rather than introducing distinctive methods of inquiry. Environmental criticism cannot claim the methodological originality, not only in literary studies but also throughout the human sciences. New critical formalism or deconstruction injected new methods of analysis in literary studies.

Environmental has made great achievements. It has offered a characteristic way of reading literary texts. It has foregrounded neglected genres like, nature writing or toxification narrative. It has changed the subject or archive. By introducing the change in the subject matter, it has revolutionized the field of critical theory. Feminism or black studies have made serious inquiry in the domain. They have not brought a radical shift in critical methodology associated with the theory. All branches of natural science are relevant to the environmental criticism. Ecocriticism concentrates on the whole branches of human sciences. Environmental aesthetic perception is more plausible. Environmentalist approach should be seen as indispensable to how one reads literature. Ecocritics inquire the environmental literacy of a text, its way of situating itself locally and/or globally, its attention or inattention to the non-human sphere, or its ideological positions with regard to receptivity or opacity to social justice issues.

Methodological self-consciousness or innovation is not unimportant. Buell emphasizes that a new critical paradigm is not the be-all or end-all that it is often thought to be. Field-defining paradigms are after all made to be broken. Edward Said's *Orientalism* exposes arrogant misconstructions by European authorities on the east. He has made contribution in opening up for literary studies underexamined dynamic of manifestation. The exploration is important for both East and the West. Human imbrication in environmentality is another example of an area under-explored in literary studies before 1990. Environmentality is a crucially more important issue of global proportions than any other issue. Environmentalism has become a much more important issue in the new century.

Environmental criticism in literary studies matters also to those people who are outside the discipline. Ecocriticism has taken academics outside the classroom. Students are taken to the field. It inspires teachers and students to undertake significant creative or critical endeavours. Environmental criticism tends to signal a reformist or transformationist aspiration.

Ecocriticism has produced a challenging intellectual work in the twenty-first century. It is a constellation rather than a single titanic book or figure. It has reinforced public concern about the fate of the earth. It has established permanent concern for literary and other humanists. It has established environmentalism as a permanent concern for literary and other humanists. It opposes environmental injustice. It explores the importance of vision and imagination in changing mind, life, and policy as well as composing words, poems, and books.

REFERENCES

1. Buell, Lawrence. *The Environmental Imagination: Thoreau, Nature Writing and the Formation of American Culture*. Cambridge MA: Harvard University Press, 1995.
2. Gore, Al. *The Earth in the Balance: Forging a New Common Purpose*. London, Sterling VA: Earthscan, 2008.
3. Barry, Lopez. *Arctic Dreams: Imagination and Desire in a Northern Landscape*. New York: Knopf Doubleday Publishing Group.
4. Entrikin, Nicholas J. *The Betweenness of Place: Towards Geography of Modernity*. New York: Palgrave Macmillan, 1990.
5. Matthews, Freya. *The Ecological Self*. New York: Routledge, 1994.
6. "Poetry and Place" *Standing by Words*. Idaho: Counterpoint LIC, 2011.

7. Aldo, Leopold. *A Sand Country Alamanc*. New York: Oxford University Press, 1987.
8. Berry, Thomas. *The Dream of the Earth*. University of California Press, 1990.
9. Jonathan. *The Song of the Earth*. Harvard University Press, 2000.

5
Conclusion

The dissertation is based on three leading writers and thinkers in the field of ecocriticism. It offers a comprehensive array of perspectives on the new approach of ecological criticism. It investigates ecological values. It examines the concept of nature. It examines human perception of wilderness. It presents environmental issues in popular culture and modern literature.

Man lives in the kingdom of nature. Human beings interact with the nature. The relationship between human life and nature is organic. We cannot live outside Nature. We breathe the air, we drink the water, we eat the food, we get the inspiration from nature, we are grateful to Nature. If the environment degrades, there is the negative impact on the health of the people.

Man has also influenced Nature tremendously. Human culture and civilization developed on the strong foundation of Nature. In the beginning, Man was completely dependent on the natural resources for the livelihood. Man has made progress and evolved as the best creation of the Nature.

Biogenetic and abiogenetic factors have contributed to the change in the biosphere. The third factor of techno genetic influence has been breaking down the relationship between human and non-human life. The problem of availability of fresh water has become acute. The problem of eliminating industrial waste has become a chronic problem before the human civilization. Nature is delicate and complex. We must plan to moderate the evil effects of technology on Nature. In socialist societies the problem of environmental destruction is solved by undertaking planned development. Capitalist societies have let loose some independent industries to damage the nature. Natural crisis has influenced human physic and psyche. From the beginning man has existed in the vicinity of Nature. Man can live well if Nature is in the proper balance. Any excessive disturbing of this balance must be to the disadvantage not only of normal existence but of any existence at all, even human life. If humanity does not succeed in preventing damage to the biosphere, we will perish altogether.

Ecocriticism is a distinct critical school or movement. It is at core revolutionary. The profession of English literature previous to ecocriticism has not addressed the issue of environment in literary texts. It has experienced tremendous growth and development. It advocates for a cultural change. It examines how the narrowness of our culture's assumptions about the nature has limited our ability to envision an ecologically sustainable human society.

We read and hear about the ongoing destruction of the environment in newspapers and on television: the greenhouse effect, ozone layer depletion, deforestation, and air and water pollution. Deep ecology offers a solution to the environmental crisis through a radical shift in human consciousness. It seeks to bring a fundamental change in the way people relate with the environment. We should not think of nature as a resource to be used for human needs. Deep Ecology emerged as an influential philosophical, social, and political movement in the 1980s. It argues that the true value of nature is intrinsic and independent of its utility. It has shaped the environmental debate among leading activists and policymakers. Other disciplines such as history, philosophy, ethics, and psychology have contributed to the field of ecocriticism. William Rueckert may have been the first person to use the term ecocriticism (Barry 240). Rueckert published an essay entitled "Literature and Ecology: An Experiment in Ecocriticism." He used ecology and ecological concepts to the study of literature. Ecocriticism has strong moral and philosophical aims. Its scope has broadened rapidly from nature narratives, romantic poetry, canonical literature, to films, theatres, television, architecture, animal stories, scientific narratives, and extraordinary range of literary texts. Ecocriticism has borrowed methodologies liberally from other fields of literature, sociology, and scientific study.

Ecocriticism has clear ethical commitments for the protection of nature. It critiques the cultural norms of the society which contribute to the environmental degradation. Camilo Gomides has defined ecocriticism: "The field of enquiry that analyzes and promotes works of art which raise moral questions about human interactions with nature, while also motivating audiences to live within a limit that will be binding over generations." It engages with the issues of resource allocation that have no technical solution. Ecocriticism explores the way texts reflect humanity's interaction with the natural world. It analyses texts as manifestations of how a culture feels towards its physical environment. It examines how humans and other elements of the ecosystem are treated in the literary text. It probes human and non-human relationship. *The Ecocriticism Reader: Landmarks in Literary Ecology* is the first collection of critical essays on nature. It is an anthology of classic and cutting-edge writings on in the rapidly emerging field of ecocriticism. It explores the relationship between literature and the physical environment. It is engaged with our most pressing contemporary problem—the global environmental crisis.

Location of the human and non-human life forms in the Nature makes their existence possible. There never was and is any life from without any place. Good things or bad things happen to human beings and other life forms when their bodies are located somewhere. Without particular location they cannot exist. Environment is not separate from us. We are part of the environment around us and we are the part of it. Edward Casey rightly said, "A placeless world is as unthinkable as a bodiless self." Environment makes an impact on physical as well as emotional lives of the people. Nature influences the human bodies, families and places.

Place configures subjective, social, and material dimensions of life. Physical environment mediates political, ethnic, economic, cultural, and religious formations. Silko resorts that people with deep sense of place are faithful in their intricate intimate relationships. Indian environmentalist Vandana Shiva charged, "The dominant system is merely the globalised version of a very local and parochial tradition." Physical environment influences individual and collective perception. Ecological value system is not distinct from our ethical and social value system. Natural values are not separate from aesthetic and social values. Ecocriticism reinvents the relation of human with nonhuman life forms. We must rethink class, race and gender along with Nature to grasp the complete meaning of human life. Henry David Thoreau appropriately made a statement, "I went to the woods because I wished to live deliberately." Nature has influenced art and literature to a large extent. There is the elemental harmony between all life forms. Ecocriticism has given the voice to Nature, the underprivileged, minorities and the subaltern. Ecocriticism will establish ecological value system. Capitalist culture has made the lives of billions of people worse across the globe. India has a rich cultural heritage. Ecocriticism will reintegrate our value system. We may establish a sense of harmony with Nature. Human mind can comprehend reality by close observation of Nature. Bioregionalism is a political movement. It has commitment for environmental and social progress of the universe with sustainability.

Domination and the oppression should be over. Vandana Shiva has attacked western concept of progress and capitalist market economy. She demystified concepts of development. She argues that market economy has worsened the condition of both women and children. We must know that poverty is one of the culprits of ecological crisis. Capitalism widens the gap between rich and poor. Poor people do not get access to the resources which are important for life. Mary Mellor said that deep ecology and materialism are similarly important. She said, "Humans are both cultured and natured; human-human relations are embedded in and constructed from human-nature relations" (Mellor 214). We must acknowledge the truth that human beings nor can any other life exist without the context of nature.

Cartesian ideology made people think that human life is separate from nature. This ideology of separation of human and nonhuman is the root cause of ecological, social and economic crisis which has occurred in almost every country in the world. Nature influences the social and individual life. Individual personality is moulded by natural surroundings. Human life is inextricably intertwined with the Nature.

Kamala Markandaya expressed the need to preserve nature. She explicates that human life is closely linked with nature. She argues in *Nectar in a Sieve* that callous policies are responsible for the degradation of nature and the poverty of the people. Natural degradation causes drought which has unavoidable consequences on the people who live in a specific area where it has occurred. She argues that industries pollute the atmosphere and undermine the quality of life of local residents. Nature is integral part of human culture and civilisation. With the death of nature, human culture and civilisation will come to an end on the planet. Markandaya has portrayed the contemporary India, facing the problems like ecological crisis, value crisis, social and economic breakdown. Human life cannot survive without Nature. She distrusts the advantages brought by industrialisation. Industrialization has made the life of the subaltern vulnerable. In the name of industry people of rural India are displaced. They are separated from their source of livelihood, i.e. land. Humanity's relationship with the nature is organic. Narmada struggle in India is a struggle for the protection of Nature, protection of lives of women, tribal/Adivasis, for the proper rehabilitation of the displaced people.

The first chapter takes an overview of the environmental philosophy observed in major religious texts of the world. It is also about the survey of the major trends in the critical theory in literary criticism. It introduces the arrival of ecological criticism in the last decade of twentieth century. It also deals with the Green Studies Movement. Indian environmentalist, Vandana Shiva asserts that spiritualism is a powerful force which connects people, nature and society. India has a rich spiritual heritage. She states: "Spirituality is not a western luxury, but a kind of life force, a kind of energy that links people to each other, to other life forms and to nature" (Vandana Shiva).

Bioregionalism is an ethos and a set of life practices. It seeks to achieve an ecologically sustainable coevolutionary symbiosis of human and nonhuman communities. It makes human life consciously ecocentric. It does not disallow anthropocentric concerns. It incorporates the concerns of both human and nonhuman life.

The study of literature and environment is not entirely a new thing. It has a rich heritage. Ecocriticism emerged as a coherent and organized discipline within literary studies with the publication of two landmark books in 1996, *The Ecocriticism Reader* edited by Cheryll Glotfelty and Harold Fromm, and Lawrence Buell's *The Environmental Imagination*. Ecocriticism explores the relationships between literature and the physical world. They write "Just as Feminist criticism examines language and literature from gender conscious perspective, and Marxist criticism brings an awareness of modes of production and economic class to its reading of texts, Ecocriticism takes an earth-centered approach to literary studies."

Ecocritics analyze the representation of Nature in literary texts. They ask the question how literature has affected human and non-human relationships.

Ecocriticism is cross-fertilized with art, history and philosophy. Environmental practices are integral to the cultural survival of people across the globe with their indigenenous diversity. Creativity and imagination are the powerful forces to enhance awareness of the relatedness of nature and human life. The arrival of Ecocriticism is timely and necessary as we are facing the environmental crisis. We should understand the environmental implications of the literary texts. Ecological criticism offers possible solutions for the contemporary for the correction of global environmental crisis. It investigates ecological values reflected in literary texts. He emphasized "the application of ecology and ecological concepts to the study of literature" (Reprinted in *The Ecocritism Reader*, p. 107). British Marxist critic, Raymond Williams wrote a seminal critique of pastoral literature in 1973, *The Country and the City*. He professed a green socialism. Joseph Meeker argues in *The Comedy of Survival* (1974) environmental crisis is primarily caused by the western tradition of separation of culture from nature. I reality both are interrelated, one cannot exist without the other.

Ecocritism has clear moral and philosophical aims. Ecocriticism has borrowed methods and approaches from other social, cultural and scientific fields. Literary scholars have analyzed the society and culture from the 1960s to the mid-1990s around the central term postmodernism. Globalization has become an organizing term to explore the contemporary economic, social, cultural and political structures. The term globalization has manifold meanings. It covers an immense spectrum of processes—international governance, global markets, corporate operations, new media technologies, cross-border communities, and various forms of migrations. The word globalization has increasingly been associated with negative connotations. It is associated with North American dominance, the exploitation of developing nations by multinational corporations.

The modern environmentalist movement began in the 1960s and 1970s. From its inception the movement has displayed ambivalence about global perspectives. The environmentalists have been concerned about saving the planet from the abuse of nature by followers of unsustainable policies. Individuals and communities have lost the connection with the surrounding nature and it is the fundamental reason for the ecological crisis. Al Gore wrote the important book, *An Inconvenient Truth* in 2006 to address the problem of loss of biodiversity and ecological disintegration. Sense of place has become the corner stone of environmental ethics to criticize and resist the operations of global capitalism. The modern environmentalists embrace certain forms of social and cultural internationalism but reject its economic manifestos. We can at environmental issues from several cultural angles. We should develop global perspectives to understand. Indra Sinha presented questions of cultural difference and global ethics in *Animal's People*

(2007). The narrator of the novel is different from the average reader. He does not even consider himself human. 'Animal' has been physically deformed by poison gases during an industrial accident. The novel has been set in Indian city of Khaufpur, a fictional version of Bhopal. An explosion at the Union Carbide plant in Bhopal killed over 2000 people immediately and thousands of people slowly.

Ecocriticism is one of the most vibrant fields of literary and cultural studies in the twenty-first century. It addresses the root reasons for the problems of environmental crisis, economic and social problems. It can be helpful to improve the quality of life for all people in the world.

Ecocritics believe that integrity and stability of the earth's ecosystems must be maintained for the purpose of community regeneration, social inclusion and enhancing security.

We have been living in the 21st century with anxiety for the future, amidst the problems of poverty, inequality, famine and conflicts. We must restore the quality of community life to reduce crime, fear of others. Material wealth can never replace quality life. People have forgotten the values of tradition. Social and cultural institutions are distorted. The forces of change are quick and uncontainable. The political system seems to lack the understanding of what impacts the policy of globalization, privatization and liberalization making on the lives of common people of the country. The political system, bureaucracy is in crisis. People are disillusioned with the political system and bureaucracy. People are alienated from the political system in both the developed and developing nations of the world. We must revitalize political, social, cultural and economic institutions to realize the progress and development of the society really.

Environmental enhancement and poverty annihilation are not separate things. They go together. The poor almost always live in the worst environments. We should strengthen democratic institutions to achieve environmental and social justice. Some people think that environmental is against the interests of the poor. Air pollution has contributed to an outbreak of respiratory illness. Agricultural failure because of environmental crisis has increased poverty. There is the need to integrate environmental and economic policy.

Sustainable development has become a policy objective for every nation in the world. The concept of sustainable development was first popularized by the Brundland Report, *Our Common Future* (1987).

Sustainable development means, "development which meets the needs of the present without compromising the ability of future generations to meet their own needs" (Brundland Report). United Nations Environment Programme defined sustainable development: "Improving the quality of life while living within the carrying capacity of supporting ecosystems" (*Caring for the Earth*, 1991). Nature must be protected to preserve ecosystem for the well-being of future generations. There must be integration of environmental and economic policy. 149 countries endorsed the goal of sustainable development at the United Nations 'Earth Summit' in Rio de Janeiro in 1992.

Environmental problems in India have become worst. Overall river quality has declined. Emissions of certain pollutants such as sulphur dioxide, carbon dioxide has grown. Urban air pollution has become a matter of serious concern because it damages health of the people. Human society must live within environmental limits. We do not control biophysical processes of nature. We partially can influence it. We should choose such a path of development that environmental improvement can be compatible with economic growth. We cannot continue the current trend of polluting the environment. Pollution may impair the basic life support systems of the planet.

Industrial societies must introduce original change in the economic structures. Our economic activities are based on the consumption of environmental resources. We cannot initiate the economic activities without the environmental resources. Pollution and natural resource depletion will cause huge pervasive damage to human health and quality of life. Industrial society and natural world are connected.

At national and international levels, we have to change the direction of development to address the issue of environmental crisis. We must redistribute national income to the poor. Consumption of public goods like transport will enhance quality of life. Pollution causes ill health. By destroying natural habitats, we may lose beauty, intricacy and harmony of nature. Natural crisis may entail our loss of sense of belonging to particular place. Sustainable lifestyle does not mean low standard life. It means improved standard of life. Public spending must increase on infrastructure, education, research, development and financial institutions.

Private companies in the national or the global market are driven by short-term competition. Proactive government policy can achieve the goal of sustainability. The functioning of the natural environment provides the physical framework and economic foundation for all human actions.

National income has increased substantially in both the developed and developing nations of the world. There is the considerable improvement in standards of nutrition, literacy, health, and sanitation. Fruits of development are not equally shared among the people. International economic policy has increased the number of people living in poverty. Existing economic policy generates wealth simultaneously it causes poverty. Increasing poverty adds to the problem of environmental degradation. It generates conflicts and tensions. Refugees and migrants are increased. Inequality affects security and stability of a nation however rich it may be.

Population growth is both a source and effect of poverty. It increases strain on the natural environment. By improving resource efficiency, we may reduce economy's impact on the environment. We have been living in the age of economic globalization. People in developed and developing countries are connected. Multinational corporations have been operating across the borders. International economic policy has supported the process of globalization. Foreign Direct Investment has become an easy matter because of liberalization. Really certain countries have got the benefits of free trade and globalization.

South, Korea, Taiwan and Singapore have got the benefits of economic globalization. Rapid economic growth has increased the urban middle-class living standards. Trade liberalization has not been very beneficial for most of the developing countries. Common people find it very difficult to meet the basic needs.

In many third world countries economic mismanagement, gross corruption, and unequal resource access have contributed to the worst living condition of the poor people. Political elites have neglected the interest of our own people. Globalizations and other allied factors have added misery to lives of the people.

Labour market liberalization has reduced wages. Financial policies have increased unemployment. Deregulation of markets has helped commercial producers. It has crippled the poor farmers. The path of economic globalization or trade liberalization will not eradicate poverty. It will increase it. The gap between rich and poor has increased. Low wages constitute one of the most important reasons of poverty. Presence of poverty is immoral. Poverty divides society and it leads to conflict. Human rights are abused, government becomes unstable or authoritarian. Development policy should reduce poverty, maintain the productivity of the environment and provide security to the people in their own lands. Multinational companies should be designed to promote environmental balance, to maintain wages protect security of the employees. We must rethink and reform present economic policy of globalization, liberalization and privatization.

Free trade will not bring benefits automatically to the society which has been following. By establishing controlling measures benefits of the free market will enhance. Markets should be regulated to protect social and environmental standards. Government should support disadvantaged sections of the society. Government should initiate economic policy and monitor it for the common good. Certainly, there are difficulties to change current financial institutions and their mechanisms. To change present national and international economic order of free trade and liberalization, it is necessary to solve the problem of poverty and environmental crisis. Each generation should leave to the children of the next generation a world at least as varied and energetic as the one it inherited. Dominant forces of change are upsetting human societies. They have increased insecurity of the people. Poverty has undermined the lives of people and communities. Poverty threatens life itself. Poor people cannot exercise their rights as citizens. They cannot retain their dignity as human beings. Because of poverty of the family, children suffer the most. We must value children and their rights. Inclusive development benefits all, exclusive development benefits none.

Rich have become richer and poor have become poorer. Poverty makes life bitterly hard for the people. It compels people to live desperately in inadequate accommodation.

Ecocriticism explicates the standard environmental image of the Earth. Globalisation for some is the homogenization of diverse local cultures. It is promoted and sustained by transnational culture industries based mainly in North America, Japan and Western Europe.

Environmentalist critics often target the economic aspect of globalisation. The growth of some transnational companies exceeds that of many nations. They possess a proportionate political power. Cornucopian enthusiasts for globalisation argue that this is an opportunity for poverty-stricken countries to develop economically. Some Asian and South American countries have realized the benefits of globalisation. They claim that deregulation of markets and the elimination of trade barriers will encourage international investment, give third world countries access to foreign markets and liberate domestic entrepreneurial capital leading to a circle of wealth creation and the kind of social and environmental progress seen mainly in rich countries. At the same time 'structural adjustment' policies imposed on third world countries by international financial institutions such as the World Bank can have crippling effects on existing social and environmental programmes, forcing governments to end price controls on basic goods, cut public spending, and privatize nationalized industries. Even then, the economic benefits of free market solutions may not accrue because of adverse domestic conditions, or because transnational corporations realize most of the profits from liberalized trade. Proactive government policy can achieve sustainable development. New economic policy of, liberalization, privatization and globalization has been useful to achieve development. The fruits of development have not been shared equally. The percentage of people living under poverty has increased in the world. Poverty affected the living standard of the people. Women tolerate the utmost load of poverty. This has led to vigorous anti-globalisation resistance in both first and third world countries. Sole economic growth will not eliminate poverty. Existing blueprint of economic development has been responsible for generation of wealth and causes poverty. Increasing poverty increases degradation of the environment.

We live in a global economy. Free trade has been beneficial for certain countries and for particular social groups within the country. South Korea, Hong Kong, Taiwan, Singapore have developed with free trade. The development enhanced living standard of the people. Global economy has increased poverty in majority of third world countries. People find it difficult to meet their basic needs. In many countries economic mismanagement, corruption, bad structures of landholdings, disregard of political elites for their own people have contributed to the deterioration of the people.

Growing poverty is morally wrong and dangerous. It leads to social division and conflict. It makes political system unstable. It may create dictatorial government. Human rights are abused in the condition of poverty. Inclusive economic development and social development will safeguard democracy.

Inequality damages the poor. It destroys the social cohesion. It affects the standard of living of everyone in the society. Decline of social cohesion has been responsible for the growth of crime. Without equality there can be no community. We are a community as a nation. Equality creates the atmosphere of social inclusion. Inclusion encourages shared respect and socially supportive actions. Regeneration of community is based on social inclusion. If we want to bring quality environment in the society, we have to first bring human equality. Without human equality, quality of environment cannot be protected. Well-being of every person is related with the social well-being. A person cannot make his life meaningful in isolation.

Animated democracy is the characteristic of a healthy society. Democratic form of the government should realize social justice and sustainability. Promotion of markets as the best way to distribute assets is accompanied by ridicule of government. Market forces are not capable to deal critical problems. They are not responsible for environmental protection, social cohesion, they do not reduce poverty, and they do not provide social goods. Government national or state should intervene specifically to achieve the aim of public service. Public decisions should be made for common good. Market should function within the constraints imposed by public decisions. The market should serve the needs of the society. It should not become the master of society. Government must be accountable and responsive to the public. Actions and policies of the government should reflect public interests not vested interests. Government must be capable to take a long-term view.

Government should involve the people in the making of policy and its implementation. Based on the large participation of the people, the decisions will be imaginative and vital. In the second decade of the twentieth century, it has become clear that the model of economic and social progress which has dominated the second half of the twentieth century no longer works. The problems of environmental degradation, global poverty and domestic inequality have threatened the gains which have been made. The model of development itself is self-defeating. Present pattern of growth actually generate many problems. Current patterns of growth contribute to the decline in the community life. It creates social problems. Social services enhance the quality life for the individual life. Poverty is the result of economic marginalization. Economic globalization uproots communities and destroys settled cultures. Investment in social goods enhances the quality of life.

Environmental degradation, global poverty, unemployment and inequality are intolerable in themselves. They damage people's lives. The problems damage people's lives. Environmental degradation causes ill health among the people. Because of poverty the society breaks down.

People become afraid of children's future. Globalization and deregulation of markets have made even middle-class jobs insecure.

Ecocritics believe that the world can be changed. Inequality in income should be over. Men and women should be able equally to realize their potentiality. Social cohesion should strengthen the communities in urban and rural areas. Cultural diversity should be celebrated. Provisions for social services enhance quality life for all. Successful democracy strengthens all people to participate in the decision-making and its implementation. New twenty-first century is the appropriate time to rethink and follow suitable path of development which is environment friendly, inclusive and sustainable.

Rachel Carson is a graceful author. She is the icon who launched the contemporary environmental movement. Her *Silent Spring* (1962) is known as the one of the most influential books of the twentieth century. She exposed the destruction of wildlife through the widespread use of pesticides. She became successful in creating awareness among the people about the environment. She influenced government to take initiative and evolve policies to protect environment. Widespread use of pesticides endangers both the human and wildlife. People themselves have poisoned the whole environment by making unnecessary use of pesticides. Carson describes a beautiful American town where people and wildlife live in harmony with each other. Then a mysterious blight strikes the area. People become ill, their illness puzzles the doctor. The vegetation dies, the fish die. Throughout earth's history, living things have interacted with the environment, but not changed it.

There is critical shortage of fresh water across the globe. Water is polluted by waste from many sources. Sea water cannot be used for drinking, irrigation or industry. Soil is also polluted. Without the earth's soil, there could be no plants and without plants there could be no animals of any kind. Soil depends on animal life to be replenished and nourished. Water, soil and plants create the world that sustains human and all other life forms. Nature plays a vital role in sustaining human life on earth. Chemical insecticides applied to land and water killed every conceivable kind of creature. Birds are disappearing from the surface of the earth. Public health problems increase because of unhygienic environment. Pesticides affect the people in both the short-term and long-term. Many of the chemicals which we have added to the environment Cellular oxidation is the basis of all life functions. Cells produce the energy required for life to continue.

Romanticism has made enduring influences on ecocriticism. Ecocritics follow other political schools of criticism in the formation of new critical criteria, re-interpreting and re-evaluating canonical texts, according to those criteria. Ecocriticism has brought new way of looking at literature, and it has contributed new ways of teaching literature. Ecocriticism has now reached full power. It is one of the most vibrant fields of literary and cultural study in the twenty-first century. It has originated from the study of nature writing and Romantic literature. It is deeply committed to the idea of place.

Ecocriticism is now quite well-established literary theory. It has been developing since 1990s. Ecocritics analyse the ecological, political and emotional ramifications of the environmental crisis reflected in creative works. Ecocritics express the need to diagnose the beliefs and political systems responsible for environmental crisis. It aims at diagnosis of social and moral ills. According to Matthew Arnold Culture is a defence against anarchy. In *Culture and Anarchy* (1869), Arnold said the person who seeks to affirm 'ordinary self' not the 'best self' is the enemy of culture.

In *Culture and Environment* (1933), F.R. Leavis and the school teacher Denys Thompson propose a description of unalienated labour:

> Their hands, their brains, imagination, conscience, sense of beauty and fitness—their personalities—were engaged and satisfied. Just as their master was not merely concerned

> for his profits, so they were not merely concerned for their wages. (*Culture and Environment*, p. 75)

We have lost the organic community with the living culture it embodied. It was sensitive to the natural world. It acknowledged the interdependence of different elements. Ecocriticism is not just concerned with merely economic sense of what is valuable. It offers the vision of unalienated self. It aims to recreate the sensuous relationship with a natural environment that was lost with industrialisation. It values the ecosystem services crucial for the human life. It acknowledges the human and cultural needs met by the forest. It does not see forest reductively and self-interestedly as a source of industrial raw material and personal profit.

Harold Fromm gives the warning that technology has created the fast illusion that we can control nature. The most important issue is that our unconquerable minds are dependent upon natural support systems. Linguistic and aesthetic competence ensures our interaction with nature. The interdisciplinary study of literature and environment is an exciting field. The ecopsychologist, Theodore Roszak said, "The environmental movement holds its place in history as the largest political cause ever undertaken by the human race" (Ecopsychology, 1). He suggests that there is a synergistic relation between planetary and personal well-being. According to Roszak, ecological crisis often brings with it spiritual fragmentation and psychological disaster. Ecological crisis is the product of our separation from the non-human world. Ecocriticism probes the fundamental question about the human relationship with nature.

Natural environment strengthens the mental health of the people. The ecopsychologists acknowledge that the core of the human mind is the ecological unconscious. They incorporate a postmodern concept of self which includes 'ecological self.'

Ecologists have used the word 'ecosuicide' for those people who destroy the resources they depend on for their survival. Humans are demanding more than the eco-system can supply.

Suicidal attitudes are a series of disconnections. The suicidal personality is disengaged from relationships, detached from the community of humans, aloof and deprived from all the phenomenon of nature.

Indigenous people believe that knowledge and land are intimately bound. They also experience that the natural world is alive, spiritually complete. Knowledge is the cultural heritage. The presence of the natural world is a condition for the very possibility of the knowledge. Knowledge is part of what relates human and non-human. Knowledge can be recalled or experienced at a specific place. They feel the spiritual tie between themselves and land. People are bound to the land ontologically and morally. The affiliation between human and non-human is strong. One senior Gumadji clan leader observes:

> We believe the land is all life. We are part of the land and the land is part of us. It cannot be one or the other. We cannot be separated by anything or anybody. (Yunupingu 1996, p. 16)

If people belong to a land, and land inheres in people, it cannot be alienated or disowned. The land involves in the constitution of the people. The environment is not something which surrounds people. The relation is ontologically basic. When the natural world becomes unbalanced, all within it are affected.

The Chinese philosophy includes *tian* (heaven), *dao, zhiran* (natural, spontaneous), and *wuxing* (five elements) in the discussion of the natural world. Chinese people held the view that human life is inextricably bound up with the natural world. Natural forces affect human life, has been a prominent feature of Chinese philosophy. The philosophy of Chinese correlative thinking supports the argument that changes in the natural world and events in the human world are interlocking. There is a correspondence between human communal and socio-political life and the natural processes.

There is a triple cooperation between *tian* (heaven), *di* (earth), and *ren* (man). The well-being of the universe depends on the successful cooperation of the three forces. Daoist philosophers argue that Man should not overvalue human concerns. All things are interconnected. It criticizes anthropocentricism. Confucian humanism affirms man's position with the universe as central or apical. In Daoist philosophy all forms of existence are ontologically equal. Daoist philosophy upholds an inclusive and holistic view of all forms of existence.

Dao is the term used to signify ultimate reality. It *is* the process of human self-cultivation. Artificial norms, values alienate human beings both from other human beings and from the natural context. All forms of beings are equal. Exploitation of other animals by human beings is unjustified. In the natural world no hierarchy exists. Superimposition of hierarchy on nature is misleading and arbitrary. The effect of hierarchy is negative for human beings and all other forms of existence.

There is a moral connection between human and non-human lives. Buddhism was introduced into China from India as early as 2 BCE. It emphasised on the metaphysical issues such as existence, causation, and reality. It retained still many basic features of its Indian form. Nature exists in all sentient and non-sentient.

People started to identify the importance of environmental pollution in the 1960s. Historian Lynn White Jr. (1967) wrote an article in *Science* on the historical roots of the ecological crisis. According to White, people's treatment to nature depends upon how they themselves see in relation to nature. According to White exploitative attitude is responsible for the ecological crisis. Medieval Latin Christianity taught people humankind as superior to the rest of God's creation. It advocated the view that God created nature and non-human beings to serve humanity. According to White, there is only on way to address the ecological crisis and that is to discard the view that nature has no reason to exist apart from serving humanity. Destruction of nature is the destruction of human civilisation and non-human life forms.

Thomas Derr observed that the countries where there is a religious respect for nature, people have ruthlessly exploited nature. Hindu religion strengthens respect and human treatment to nature. Human greed and exploitative tendencies have been the main cause of environmental destruction. Inter-religious and intercultural conflicts and wars have also contributed to the environmental problems. The *Prithvi Sukta* urges there should be unity amongst all races and amongst all beliefs. Abuse and exploitation of nature for selfish gain is unjust and disrespectful.

Mother Earth provides us with a sustainable environment. The *Atharva Veda* (about 2000 BCE) constitutes the concept of the respect to the earth. It is perhaps the first of its kind to express spiritual and inherent relationship between humanity and earth. Earth nourishes all beings-human and non-human. It includes the concept of *Vasudhaiv Kutumbakam.* Every entity and organism is part of a large extended family. It is presided over by the Mother Earth. One must be respectful to one's mother. One should not exploit, insult her. Hindu religion provides moral guidance for preservation and conservation of environment. Firmness, purity and fertility of the Earth are for well-being and development of all. No one nation or group has special authority over the resource of the earth. We should preserve the original fragrance of the earth. We should sustain the natural legacy of the earth for future generations.

Lord Krishna praises highly the importance of plants and other vegetation in *Bhagavad Gita.* He says that among all plants and trees, He is an *Ashvatthah*—a tree which grows anywhere, even on a very hard surface (*Bhagavad Gita*, Chapter 10, Verse 26). The *Prithvi Sukta* also mentions that natural beauty in the urban places should be preserved so that the land remains a place of worthwhile living for all. We should be gracious to the Mother Earth. Hindu religion argues for ecospirituality. The constitution of India expresses categorically the need for a healthy environment. Right to wholesome environment is the part of the right of life. Article 21 of the constitution incorporates the right to wholesome environment. The relationship between man and his environment is undergoing profound changes in the wake of modern scientific and technological developments. In our country various laws have been enacted to protect environment.

Environmental protection and improvement were explicitly incorporated in the Indian constitution by the Forty-second

Amendment Act of 1976. It declares: "The State shall endeavour to protect and improve the environment and to safeguard the forest and wildlife of the country." Human activities have threatened the survival of world's plant and animal life. A healthy environment provides humans with social, economic, scientific, educational and cultural benefits. There is the intrinsic relationship between people and their environment. Protection of the environment includes the protection of health, life and cultural integrity of the people. Every person has the right to live in a clean, healthy and adequate environment. Environmental sustainability is a prerequisite for poverty reduction and development.

We must develop a responsible approach to the environment. We must take bold, visionary steps to confront the environmental crisis. If we do not address the problem of crisis adequately, future generations will not forgive us. We should not assume that everything in nature is limitless and free. We should bring transformation in our thoughts and behaviour to the extent necessary to save the environment.

Some self-interested cynics tell that global warming is not a problem. Civilisation has now reached mature configuration. The people who have the vested interests in the status quo, do not want to bring a meaningful change. Institutions like family are uprooted. We must preserve the values which nurture our concern for future.

Environmentally appropriate technologies will be of immense help in the achievement of sustainable development. Ecologically destructive technologies in use should be replaced. Technology alone is not the solution over the ecological problems. We should understand both the potential and danger of technology. Simply more technology addition will degrade the problem. We should redefine our relationship to the environment. Crisis can be solved if we approach it holistically. Problems are related to one another. Education programme, economic, social and political inclusion of the people will largely help to address problem of environmental crisis.

According to Jefferson, healing the environment represents a renewed dedication to the universal inalienable rights, life, liberty, and the pursuit of happiness. The real enemy is the dysfunctional way of thinking. Alienation and technology go together. The new ideology of consumption collapses the individual into the desire for what they consume. It fosters the assumption that we are separate from the earth. It is this eccentric and destructive way of thinking about our relationship to the nature is our real enemy.

To save environment is to protect true freedom and human dignity. National governments should show deep respect for the political and economic freedom of the individuals.

Ecologically oriented literary critics and theorists can play a constructive role in scientific progress. Literature studies for the insights into the human nature. Ecocriticism constructs bridges across the abyss between the two cultures of science and humanities. It challenges anthropocentricism. We must establish creative relationships to animals. The deepest commitment of ecocriticism is to the notion of place or locale.

Ecocriticism is also engaged with the mainstream film. It has analysed movies thematically, in the same manner of analyzing a literary text. The material, social and perceptual ecology of every film has been analysed by the ecocritics. Ecocritics examine the direct and indirect environmental impact of a particular production. They consider its political and cultural impacts. Perceptual ecology deals with the production of places and non-human life forms.

David Orr has observed, all education is already environmental. Teaching practices have ecological impacts. Educational explicit and unseen curricula carry ecological meanings and implications. Ecocritical pedagogy makes its existing environmentality explicit and sustainable.

Ecocritics perceive world as a evolutionary ecosystem in which line of connections extend to all directions. Different creatures and elements are reshaping the world they inhabit—their local ecosystem and beyond it the global ecosystem or biosphere. Ecological approach to culture explores the interconnection between the human life and the physical life. Ecocriticism is an environmentalist version of English studies. It is quite well established and has been developing since the 1990s. Ecocritics follow other political forms of criticism in formulating new critical criteria. They reinterpret and re-evaluate canonical texts according to those criteria. They analyse the concepts such as 'nature', 'wilderness', 'humanity', 'the animal', and 'progress.' Attitudes are originated in culture. Attitude has been largely responsible for the present ecological crisis. Ecocritics explore the ecological, political and emotional ramifications of the environmental crisis. They develop future environmental scenarios. They oppose industrial instrumentalist rationality. They diagnose the beliefs and political systems responsible for environmental crisis. Diagnosis of social and moral ills will eliminate the ecological crisis.

Ecocriticism has brought new ways of looking at literature. It has offered new methods of teaching in the classrooms. Arnold describes in *Culture and Anarchy* (1869) that one who seeks to affirm his or her 'ordinary self' is the enemy of culture. According to Arnold inward perfection should be the goal of an individual. In *Culture and Environment* (1933), F.R. Leavis and Denys Thompson have offered a description of unalienated labour:

> Their hands their brains, imagination, conscience, sense of beauty and fitness—their personalities—were engaged and satisfied. Just as their master was not merely concerned for his profits, so they were not merely concerned for their wages. (Leavis and Thompson, p. 75)

The organic social culture is always sensitive to the natural world. The different elements of society are interdependent. Rituals and symbols in the culture renew traditional environmental knowledge. Ecocritics explore the modern consumerism which has created many economic and social problems. We should not be satisfied with the economic sense of what is valuable but we must develop the environmental sense of what is valuable. We should re-establish the sensuous relationship with the environment which once we had. With the advent of industrialisation, we have lost the cherished relationship with the environment.

Education is redefined as a private and personal good. Nussbaum remarked that dullness and trained submissiveness threatens the very spirit of democracy. Humanities' scholars resist the commodification of education which undermines the social spirit. Conceptions of personal and public good are neglected.

Cheryll Glotfelty is an Associate Professor of literature and the environment at the University of Nevada, Reno. Harold Fromm is author of *Academic Capitalism and Literary Value*. He is an independent scholar and visiting professor of English at the University of Illinois, Chicago.

According to Cheryll Glotfelty ecocriticism is the study of the relationship between human life and the environment. *The Ecocriticism Reader: Landmarks in Literary Ecology* is the first collection of its kind, an anthology of classic and cutting-edge writings in the rapidly emerging field of ecological criticism. It is edited by Cheryll Glotfelty and Harold Fromm. It defines ecological literary discourse. It presents the development of ecocriticism. It provides appealingly and lucidly written examples of the range of ecological approaches to literature. There is the apparent connection between literature and the environment.

Environmental perspective in contemporary literary study has become relevant and significant because of global environmental crisis. Literary scholars have responded to the present environmental crisis. Ecological critics argue that human culture is connected to the physical world, affecting it and affected by it. Ecocriticism studies the relationship between nature and culture. Contemporary psychologists acknowledge that the modern estrangement from nature is the basis of our social and psychological ills. Race, class and gender were the hot topics of the twentieth century. Earth's life support systems are under stress. Space has become a new critical category.

Ecocriticism studies the representation of nature in fiction and drama. Technology has created the fast illusion that we can control nature. We are dependent for our survival and development on nature. Man's unnatural treatment of nature has brought sad results. Today we should promote an understanding of, and reverence for nature. We must promote an ecological vision. The ecological vision must penetrate the economic, political, social and technological visions of our time. Reinterpretation and reformation of literary canon has arrived with the ecocriticism, which has close links with the public life. We must acknowledge that Nature is the symbol for order and glory of God. Nature spiritualizes human life.

Harold Fromm is a visiting scholar at the University of Arizona. He writes on self, environment and academia. He is the co-editor of *The Ecocriticism Reader* and the author of *Academic Capitalism and Literary Value.*

There is the close relationship between human life and nature, and it reflects in literature. There is the connection between the environment in which we live and our creativity. Our consciousness is bounded and delimited by our materiality.

Harold Fromm explores the views of nature. He argues for the naturalistic vision of creativity. We should think about our place in the environment. Fromm has explicated three main movements, ecology, Darvinism and Consciousness studies in *The Nature of Being Human: From Environmentalism to Consciousness.*

Lawrence Buell is Professor of English at Harvard University. He is best known for his two previous books on environmental criticism, *The Environmental Imagination* (1995) and *Writing for an Endangered World* (2001). His book on Emerson was also widely admired. He is author of *The Environmental Imagination: Thoreau, Nature Writing, and the Formation of American Culture.*

Lawrence Buell is one of the leading theorists in ecocriticism. He traces the ecocritical movement back to 1970s. Ecocriticism has arrived as an independent critical theory in the 1990s. He wrote *The Future of Environmental Criticism: Environmental Crisis and Literary Imagination.* This manifesto summarizes the critical practices in ecocriticism.

Lawrence Buell is the winner of the 2001 John G. Cawelti Award sponsored by The Popular Culture Association and American Culture Association for the best book in the field of American culture studies. The environmental imagination does not stop short at the edge of the woods and nature. Lawrence Buell makes it clear that the ecocriticism theory has reshaped the field of literature and environment.

Ecocriticism is one of the important theories in the twenty-first century. It also deals with the issues of social justice and equity. Nature matters for the survival and development of human and non-human life. We should realize that human life is embedded in the environment. All organisms including human life are part of a larger biotic web or network of community whose interest must constrain or direct or govern the human interest. Ecocriticism might also provide the foundation for reorganization of political, economic, cultural and social life. Ecocriticism has strengthened the close association of human life and nature. It asks the elemental questions of ourselves and literature.

Ecocriticism aims to enhance the values of the human communities and the natural world. All life is precious, human and non-human life. We are the part of the natural world. Human life flourishes within the intricate and interdependent web/network of life. Political pollution of corruption is an evil responsible for damaging the earth's life support systems and human life. The promotion of justice and protection of the environment are interdependent. Ecocriticism explores the issues of social and environmental justice. It is prominent critical theory in literature.

Bibliography

Primary Sources

Buell, Lawrence. *The Environmental Imagination: Thoreau, Nature Writing, and the Formation of American Culture*. Cambridge, MA and London, England: Harvard University Press, 1995.

——. *Emerson*. London: The Belknap Press of Harvard University Press, 2011.

——. *The Environmental Imagination: Thoreau, Nature Writing, and the Formation of American Culture*. Cambridge: Harward University Press, 1995.

——. *The Future of Environmental Criticism: Environmental Crisis and Literary Imagination*. Oxford: Blackwell, 2005.

——. *Writing for an Endangered World: Literature, Culture, and Environment in the U.S. and Beyond*. Cambridge, MA and London, England: The Belknap Press of Harvard University Press, 2001.

—— ed. *The American Transcendentalists: Essential Writings*. New York: Modern Library, 2006.

Fromm, Harold. *The Nature of Being Human: From Environmentalism to Consciousness*. Baltimore: Johns Hopkins University Press, 2009.

——. *Academic Capitalism and Literary Value*. Athens GA: University of Georgia Press, 1991.

Glotfelty, Cheryll and Fromm, Harold eds. *The Ecocriticism Reader: Landmarks in Literary Ecology*. Athens and London: University of Georgia, 1996.

Secondary Sources

Adamson, Joni, Mei Evans and Rachel Stein eds. *The Environmental Justice Reader: Politics, Poetics, and Pedagogy*. Tucson: University of Arizona Press, 2002.

Ahmad, Aijaz. *In Theory: Classes, Nations Literatures*. New York: Verso, 2008.

Armbruster, Karla, and Kathleen R. Wallace. *Beyond Nature Writing: Expanding the Boundaries of Ecocriticism*. London: University Press of Virginia, 2008.

Arnold, Matthew. *Culture and Anarchy*. New Haven: Yale University Press (1869), 1994.

Barry, Peter. *Beginning Theory: An Introduction to Literary and Cultural Theory*. 3rd ed. Manchester: Manchester University Press, 2009.

Bate, Jonathan. *The Song of the Earth*. London: Picador, 2000.

——. *Romantic Ecology: Wordsworth and the Environmental Tradition*, London: Routledge, 1991.

Beck, Ulrich. *Risk Society: Towards a New Modernity*. Trans. Mark Ritter. London: Sage, 1992.

——. *Ecological Politics in an Age of Risk*. Trans. Amos Weiz. Cambridge: Polity Press, 1995.

Berry, Thomas. *The Dream of the Earth*. San Francisco: Sierra Club, 1988.

Berry, Wendell. *A Continuous Harmony: Essays Cultural and Agricultural*. San Diego, CA: Harcourt, 1972.

——. *Home Economics*. Berkeley, CA: North Point, 1987.

Bhabha, Homi. *The Location of Culture*. London: Routledge, 1994.

Botkin, Daniel B. *Discordant Harmonies: A New Ecology for the Twenty First Century*. New York: Oxford University Press, 1990.

Carson, Rachel. *Silent Spring*. London: Penguin, 2000.

——. *Under the Sea Wind*.

Chand, Devi. Trans. *Yajurveda*. New Delhi: Munshiram Manoharlal Publishers, 1982.

Cheng, C.Y. "The Origins of Chinese Philosophy," ed. B. Carr and I. Mahalingam. *Companion Encyclopedia of Asian Philosophy*. London: Routledge, 1997.

Cheng, W.T. *A Source Book in Chinese Philosophy*. Princeton: Princeton University Press, 1961.

Coetzee, J.M. *Disgrace*. New York: Viking, 1999.

Coupe, Lawrence. Ed. *The Green Studies Reader: From Romanticism to Ecocriticism*. London: Routledge, 2000.

Cronon, William. Ed. *Uncommon Ground: Rethinking the Human Place in Nature*. New York: W.W. Norton, 1995.

Datta, M.N. trans. *Mahabharata*. Delhi: Parimal Publications, 1988.

Dennett, Daniel. *Sweet Dreams: Philosophical Obstacles to a Science of Consciousness*. Cambridge: MIT Press, 2005.

Duerr, Peter Hans. *Dreamtime: Concerning the Boundary Between Wilderness and Civilisation*. Trans. Goodman Felicitas. Oxford: Basil Blackwell, 1985.

Dwivedi, O.P. *Ethics of Environment and Development: Global Challenge and International Response*, eds. J. Ronald Engel and Joan Gibbs Engel. London: Belhaven Press, 1990.

Edelman, Gerald M. *Wider Than the Sky: The Phenomenal Gift of Consciousness*. New Haven: Yale University Press, 2004.

Edward, Abbey. *Desert Solitaire: A Season in the Wilderness*. New York: Ballantine, 1968.

Ehrenfeld, David. *The Arrogance of Humanism*. Oxford: Oxford University Press, 1978.

Ferry, Luc. *The New Ecological Order*. Trans. Carol Volk. Chicago: University of Chicago Press, 1995.

Foreman, Dave. *Confessions of an Eco-Warrior*. New York: Harmony Books, 1999.

Foucault, Michel. *The Order of Things: An Archaeology of the Human Sciences*. New York: Vintage Press, 1973.

Gaard, G., Murphy, P.D. eds. *Ecofeminist Literary Criticism: Theory, Interpretation, Pedagogy*. Urbana IL: University of Illinois Press, 1998.

Gadgil, Madhav and Ramchandra Guha. *Ecology and Equity: The Use and Abuse of Nature in Contemporary India*. London: Routledge, 1995.

Garrard, Greg. *Ecocriticism*. 2nd ed. London: Routledge, 2011.

Glotfelty, Cheryll, Tom Lynch, Karla Armbruster eds. *The Bioregional Imagination: Literature, Ecology, and Place*. Athens: University of Georgia Press, 2012.

Glotfelty, Cheryll. *Literary Nevada: Writings from the Silver State*. Reno: University of Nevada Press, 2008.

Gore, Al. *Earth in the Balance: Forging a New Common Purpose*. London, Sterling: EARTHSCAN, 2008.

Gore, Al. *Earth in the Balance: Forging a New Common Purpose*. London: Earthscan, 1992.

——. *An Inconvenient Truth: The Global Emergency of Global Warming and What We can Do about It*. New York: Rodale, 2006.

Goswami, C.L. and Shastri, M.A. Trans. *Srimad Bhagavata Mahapurana*. Gorakhpur: Gita Press, 1982.

Greenblatt, Stephen and Gunn Giles eds. *Redrawing the Boundaries: The Transformation of English and American Literary Studies*. New York: MLA, 1992.

Griffin, Susan. *Woman and Nature: The Roaring Inside Her*. New York: *Harper*, 1978.

Haraway, Donna. *When Species Meet*. Minneapolis: University of Minnesota Press, 2007.

Heise, Ursula. *Sense of Place and Sense of Planet: The Environmental Imagination of the Global*. New York: Oxford University Press, 2008.

Jacobs, Michael. *The Politics of the Real World*. London: Earthscan, 1998.

Jamieson, Dale. *A Companion to Environmental Philosophy*. Berlin: Blackwell Publishing, 2003.

Jefferson, Thomas. *Notes on the State of Virginia*. London, 1785.

Kroeber, Karl. *Ecological Literary Criticism: Romantic Imagining and the Biology of Mind*. New York: Columbia University Press, 1994.

Leavis F.R. and Denys Thompson. *Culture and Environment: The Training of Critical Awareness*. London: Chatto & Windus, 1933.

Leopold, Aldo. *A Sand Country Almanac*. New York: Oxford University Press, 1987.

——. *The River of the Mother of God and Other Essays*. Ed. Susan I. Flader and J. Baird Callicot. Madison: University of Wisconsin Press, 1991.

Love, Glen A. *Practical Ecocriticism: Literature, Biology, and the Environment*. Charlottesville: University of Virginia Press, 2003.

Marx, Leo. *The Machine in the Garden: Technology and the Pastoral Ideal in America*. Oxford: Oxford University Press, 1964.

Mathews, Freya. *Reinhabiting Reality: Towards a Recovery of Culture*. New York: State University of New York Press, 2005.

——. *The Ecological Self*. Savage MD: Barnes and Noble, 1991.

Mazel, D. *A Century of Ecocriticism*. Athens G.A.: University of Georgia Press, 2001.

Meeker, Joseph. *The Comedy of Survival: Studies in Literary Ecology*. New York: Scribner's, 1972.

Merchant, Carolyn. *Radical Ecology: The Search for a Livable World*. New York: Routledge, 1992.

——. *The Death of Nature: Women, Ecology and the Scientific Revolution*. San Francisco: HarperCollins, 1980.

——. *Ecological Revolutions: Nature, Gender, and Science in New England*. Chapel Hill: University of North Carolina Press, 1989.

——. Ed. *Ecology*. Amherst, NY: Humanity Books, 1999.

Morton, T. *The Ecological Thought*. Cambridge M.A.: Harvard University Press, 2010.

Nash, Roderick Frazier. *The Rights of Nature.* Madison: University of Wisconsin Press, 1989.

Nussbaum, M.C. and Cohen, J. eds. *For Love of Country: Debating the Limits of Patriotism.* Boston: Beacon Press, 1996.

Orr, D. *Ecological Literacy: Education and the Transition to a Postmodern World.* Albany: State University of New York Press, 1992.

Palmer, J. *Environmental Education in the 21st Century.* London: Routledge, 1998.

Phillips, Dana. *The Truth of Ecology: Nature, Culture, and Literature in America.* Oxford: Oxford University Press, 2003.

Pickett, S., Kolasa, J. and Jones, C. *Ecological Understanding: The Nature of Theory and the Theory of Nature.* Amsterdam: Elsevier, 2007.

Plumwood, V. *Environmental Culture.* London: Routledge, 2001.

——. *Feminism and the Mastery of Nature.* London: Routledge, 1993.

——. *Reinventing Eden: The Fate of Nature in Western Culture.* New York: Routledge, 2004.

Rich, Adrienne. *Atlas of the Difficult World: Poems 1988-1991.* New York: W.W. Norton, 1992.

Rueckert, William. "Literature and Ecology: An Experiment in Ecocriticism." *Iowa Review*, 9.1 (1978): 71-86.

Said, Edward. *Orientalism.* New York: Random House, 1978.

——. *Culture and Imperialism.* New York: Knoff, 1993.

——. *The World, The Text, and the Critic.* Cambridge, MA: Harvard University Press, 1983.

Saraswati, Maharishi Dayanand. Trans. *Rig Veda.* New Delhi: Servadeshik Arya Pratinidhi Sabha, 1974.

Selvamony, Nirmal, Nirmaldasan and Rayson, K. Alex. *Essays in Ecocriticism.* Delhi: Sarup and Sons and OSLE-India, 2008.

Shiva, Vandana. *Staying Alive: Women, Ecology and Development*. London: Zed Books, 1989.

Showalter, Elaine. Ed. *The Feminist Criticism: Essays on Women, Literature, and Theory*. New York: Pantheon, 1985.

Sinha, Indra. *Animal's People*. New York: Simon and Schuster, 2007.

Skolimowski, Henryk. *Eco-philosophy*. Boston: Marion Boyers, 1973.

Slovic, Scott. *Going Away to Think*. Reno: University of Nevada Press, 2008.

Slovic, Scott. *Seeking Awareness in American Nature Writing: Henry Thoreau, Annie Dillard, Edward Abbey, Wendell Berry, Barry Lopez*. Salt Lake City, UT: University of Utah Press, 1992.

Smith, Neil. *Uneven Development: Nature, Capital and the Production of Space*. Oxford: Blackwell, 1984.

Snow, C.P. *The Two Cultures and the Scientific Revolution*. New York: Cambridge University Press, 1959.

Soper, Kate. *What is Nature?* Oxford: Blackwell, 1998.

Stiglitz, Joseph. *Globalisation and Its Discontents*. New Delhi: Penguin Books, 2003.

——. *The Price of Inequality: How Today's Divided Society Endangers Our Future*. New Delhi: Penguin Books, 2012.

Thomashow, Mitchell. *Bringing the Biosphere Home. Learning Perceive Global Environmental Change*. London: MIT Press, 2002.

——. *Ecological Identity: Becoming a Reflective Environmentalist*. Cambridge: MIT Press, 1995.

Thoreau, Henry. *The Maine Woods*. Princeton: Princeton University Press, 1983.

——. *Walden*. London: Dent, 1992.

Tilak, Bal Gangadhar. *Gita Rahasya*. Poona: Tilak Brothers, 1936.

Wagge, Frederick O. ed. *Teaching Environmental Literature: Materials, Methods, Resources*. New York: Modern Language Association, 1985.

Wegner, Daniel. *The Illusion of Conscious Will*. Cambridge: MIT Press, 2002.

White, Jr., Lynn. "The historical roots of our ecological crisis." *Science*, 155, pp. 1203-07, 1967.

Williams, Raymond. *The Country and the City*. London: Chatto and Windus, 1973.

Willms, Johannes. *Conversations with Ulrich Beck*. Trans. Michael Pollak. Cambridge: Polity Press, 2004.

Wilson, E.O. *Consilience: The Unity of Knowledge*. New York: Random House, 1998.

World Commission on Environment and Development. *Our Common Future*. Oxford: Oxford University Press, 1987.

Worster, Donald. *The Wealth of Nature: Environmental History and the Ecological Imagination*. New York: Oxford University Press, 1993.

——. *Nature's Economy: A History of Ecological Ideas*. Cambridge: Cambridge University Press, 1977.

Wright, Judith. *Going on Talking*. Springwood, NSW: Butterfly Books, 1992.

Yunupingu, G. *Our Land is Our Life*. Queensland: University of Queens land Press, 1997.

Webliography

http://en.wikipedia.org/wiki/Ecocriticism

http://www.asle.org/site/resources/ecocritical-lit

http://ojs.unbc/ca/index.php/joe

http://www.easlce.eu/about-us/what-is-ecocriticism

http://www.stanford.edu/-uheise

http://www.ucpress.edu

http://www.yale.edu

http://www.jacketflap.com/dodo-press publisher

http://bookdepository.co.uk
http://www.raptisrarebooks.com
www.flipkart.com
http://victorianweb.org/author/eliot
http://www.palgrave.com/online resources
http://www.amazon.com
http://www.jstor.org/action/show publisher